Past Masters

J. O. Urmson is an Emeritus Professor of Stanford
University and an Emeritus Fellow of Corpus
Christi College, Oxford. He is the author of
*Philosophical Analysis, The Emotive Theory of
Ethics, Aristotle's Ethics,* and *The Greek
Philosophical Vocabulary,* and editor of *The
Encyclopedia of Western Philosophy.*

Past Masters

AQUINAS Anthony Kenny
ARISTOTLE Jonathan Barnes
ARNOLD Stefan Collini
AUGUSTINE Henry Chadwick
BACH Denis Arnold
FRANCIS BACON Anthony Quinton
BAYLE Elisabeth Labrousse
BENTHAM John Dinwiddy
BERGSON Leszek Kolakowski
BERKELEY J. O. Urmson
THE BUDDHA Michael Carrithers
BURKE C. B. Macpherson
CARLYLE A. L. Le Quesne
CERVANTES P. E. Russell
CHAUCER George Kane
CLAUSEWITZ Michael Howard
COBBETT Raymond Williams
COLERIDGE Richard Holmes
CONFUCIUS Raymond Dawson
DANTE George Holmes
DARWIN Jonathan Howard
DESCARTES Tom Sorell
DIDEROT Peter France
GEORGE ELIOT Rosemary Ashton
ENGELS Terrell Carver
ERASMUS James McConica
FREUD Anthony Storr
GALILEO Stillman Drake
GIBBON J. W. Burrow
GOETHE T. J. Reed
HEGEL Peter Singer
HOBBES Richard Tuck
HOMER Jasper Griffin
HUME A. J. Ayer

KIERKEGAARD Patrick Gardiner
JESUS Humphrey Carpenter
KANT Roger Scruton
LAMARCK L. J. Jordanova
LEIBNIZ G. MacDonald Ross
LOCKE John Dunn
MACHIAVELLI Quentin Skinner
MALTHUS Donald Winch
MARX Peter Singer
MENDEL Vitezslav Orel
MILL William Thomas
MONTAIGNE Peter Burke
MONTESQUIEU Judith N. Shklar
THOMAS MORE Anthony Kenny
WILLIAM MORRIS Peter Stansky
MUHAMMAD Michael Cook
NEWMAN Owen Chadwick
PAINE Mark Philp
PASCAL Alban Krailsheimer
PAUL E. P. Sanders
PETRARCH Nicholas Mann
PLATO R. M. Hare
PROUST Derwent May
RUSKIN George P. Landow
SCHILLER T. J. Reed
SHAKESPEARE Germaine Greer
ADAM SMITH D. D. Raphael
SPINOZA Roger Scruton
TOLSTOY Henry Gifford
VICO Peter Burke
VIRGIL Jasper Griffin
WITTGENSTEIN A. C. Grayling
WYCLIF Anthony Kenny

Forthcoming

JOSEPH BUTLER R. G. Frey
COPERNICUS Owen Gingerich
DURKHEIM Frank Parkin
GODWIN Alan Ryan
JOHNSON Pat Rogers
LINNAEUS W. T. Stearn
NEWTON P. M. Rattansi
NIETZSCHE Ernst Behler

ROUSSEAU Robert Wokler
RUSSELL A. C. Grayling
SOCRATES Bernard Williams
TOCQUEVILLE Larry Siedentop
MARY WOLLSTONECRAFT
    William St Clair
and others

J. O. Urmson

BERKELEY

Oxford   New York
OXFORD UNIVERSITY PRESS

Oxford University Press, Walton Street, Oxford OX2 6DP

Oxford New York Toronto
Delhi Bombay Calcutta Madras Karachi
Petaling Jaya Singapore Hong Kong Tokyo
Nairobi Dar es Salaam Cape Town
Melbourne Auckland

and associated companies in
Berlin Ibadan

Oxford is a trade mark of Oxford University Press

First published 1982 as an Oxford University Press paperback
Reprinted 1991

British Library Cataloguing in Publication Data

Urmson, J. O.
Berkeley.—(Past masters)
1. Berkeley, George
I. Title II. Series
192 B1348
ISBN 0-19-287546-9

Library of Congress Cataloging in Publication Data
Data available

Printed in Great Britain by
Biddles Ltd.
Guildford and King's Lynn

Contents

Note on abbreviations

The following abbreviations are used in references to Berkeley's works:

A *Alciphron*
C *Philosophical Commentaries*
L *The Works of George Berkeley*, ed. Luce and Jessup (see p. 88)
M *De motu*
O *Passive Obedience*
P *Principles of Human Knowledge*
S *Siris*
V *A New Theory of Vision*

References to L are by volume and page, references to A, M, O, P, S and V by paragraph. References to C follow the numbering (not Berkeley's) adopted in L i.

1 The corpuscularian philosophy

At some time not precisely known, but certainly when he was in his very early twenties, if not earlier, George Berkeley, newly graduated B.A. of Trinity College, Dublin, had a metaphysical inspiration. It was one which seemed to him, on reflection, to be blindingly obvious; it served as a basis for answers to at least most of the outstanding problems of metaphysics; it removed the temptation to scepticism and atheism presented by current philosophical orthodoxy; it preserved, perhaps in a more sophisticated form, everything that either common sense or the revelations of the Christian religion maintained. This new insight was that there was no such thing as matter, that the concept of matter was totally superfluous and even unintelligible.

So stated, baldly, out of context and without explanation, this alleged insight will presumably appear utterly ridiculous to the reader not already acquainted with Berkeley's thought. It appeared utterly ridiculous to, for example, Dr Johnson, who believed, ignorantly but not unnaturally, that he could refute it by kicking a stone. One of the principal aims of this book will be to show the reader how, in the context of the philosophical and scientific beliefs of his time, Berkeley's thesis was a very rational one to adopt, and to show how ingeniously Berkeley developed it within the bounds of one of the most elegant, clear and simple metaphysical systems ever devised. The reader will not be asked to accept the doctrine, though some philosophers do accept it; but he should come to see that it is the work of one of the world's great philosophical geniuses and worthy of admiring study.

To understand how Berkeley came to propound this, at first sight, absurd and irresponsible thesis we must first have some acquaintance with the philosophical and scientific outlook of the vast majority of seventeenth-century thinkers against which Berkeley was revolting.

The seventeenth century, towards the close of which Berkeley was born, saw the birth of modern experimental science.

Broadly speaking, for the historian of science will easily cite counter-examples to the generalization, scientific investigation had ceased during the dark and middle ages. Already during the Renaissance it was beginning to revive. But it was at the beginning of the seventeenth-century that Galileo set out to establish the main principles of statics and made a beginning in dynamics, the two main branches of the great science of mechanics which had been largely neglected since Archimedes and which Newton was by the century's end to bring to a perfection which for two further centuries seemed to be final. Galileo also developed the microscope and the telescope, the indispensable tools for the investigation of the minute and the distant. Between him and Newton came Harvey, the Dutch mathematician Snell, Descartes, the Italian physicist Torricelli, Pascal, Sydenham, Boyle, Huygens, Hooke; great academies of science, including the Royal Society of London, were instituted; kings and nobility, including Charles II, had their own experimental laboratories; to many it seemed that all the secrets of nature would before long be revealed, though by the end of the century this optimism had waned.

Underlying and partly determining this burst of scientific activity was a new philosophical outlook which had replaced the scholasticism of the past few centuries. It was called sometimes the modern philosophy and sometimes the corpuscularian philosophy. Largely through the agency of the Frenchman Peter Gassendi (1592–1655), classical scholar, astronomer and general intellectual factotum, a knowledge of the ancient atomic hypothesis of Democritus and Epicurus was revived, and this ontology of atoms and the void quickly won acceptance. Enthusiasm for it broke through even in a report to the puritan government of the Protectorate on the state of the English Universities; in his *Examination of Academies* John Webster wrote in 1654: 'What shall I say of the Epicurean philosophy, brought to light, illustrated and completed by the labour of that general scholar Petrus Gassendus? Surely if it be rightly examined it will prove a more perfect and sound piece than any the Schools ever had or followed.' Though Descartes and his followers could not accept the void they enthusiastically subscribed to the ideal of mechanistic explanation, and a Catholic eclectic like Sir

Kenelm Digby could write that all could be explained by particles 'working by local motion'.

This 'modern philosophy' became the theoretical foundation of science in England. The truly magnificent title of a book by Henry Power, Dr of Physick, published in 1664, *Experimental Philosophy in Three Books, containing New Experiments Microscopical, Mercurial, Magnetical with some deductions and probable Hypotheses raised from them in avouchment and illustration of the now famous Atomical Hypothesis*, well illustrates the mood of the times.

What, then, was this modern philosophy, the corpuscularian philosophy, which Dr Power called the atomical hypothesis? Since we are constantly informed by ignorant persons that the ancient Greeks had a merely speculative atomic fantasy whereas the modern atomic theory was founded on solid experimental observation, any resemblance being coincidental, it would be as well to say again that the corpuscularian philosophy simply is the ancient Greek theory revived and is clearly stated to be so by its main proponents. Since it was to be the main target of Berkeley's criticism, a theory which he regarded as the fountain of all error, we had better become quite closely acquainted with it. Berkeley had studied it carefully.

The corpuscularian philosophy held that the world consisted of atoms in motion in an infinite void; in the ancient version the atoms so moved in infinite time, but the Christian philosophers of the seventeenth-century accepted, on the authority of the Bible, that they were created and set in motion by God. Thus Newton, in Query 30 to his *Optics*, said: 'It seems probable to me that God in the beginning formed matter in solid, massy, hard, impenetrable, movable particles, of such sizes and figures, and with such other properties and in such proportion to space as most conduced to the end for which he formed them.' These atoms were considered to be of many different shapes and sizes, solid, indestructible and in motion.

But if we ask with what other properties God endowed the atoms, the answer will be: 'None.' 'Hot and cold are appearance, sweet and bitter are appearance, colour is appearance; in reality there are the atoms and the void' said Democritus in one of the few surviving fragments of his scientific writings, and with this the seventeenth-century scientists entirely agreed. The corpuscularian philosophy is a theory of pure mechanism.

Everything is to be explained in terms of the shape, size, mass and motion of the particles and their impact on each other; in other words, mechanical explanation is the only acceptable form of scientific explanation. Impact was the only way in which anything could be conceived to act on anything else. This was agreed on all hands; thus Locke, in Book II of his *An Essay concerning Human Understanding*, spoke of 'impulse, the only way which we can conceive bodies operate in', and even the arch-rationalist Leibniz (1646–1716), commenting on this passage of Locke, says: 'I also am of the opinion that bodies act only by impulse.' So what was explicable was ultimately to be explained mechanically; what could not be so explained was not scientifically explicable at all and had to be referred to the direct decrees of God.

This insistence on mechanical explanation cannot be overemphasised. It can be illustrated by reference to the theory of gravitation. Newton had discovered the famous law that bodies tend to move towards each other with an acceleration proportional to the product of the masses and inversely proportional to the square of the distance between them. It might seem that here is an example of a force of attraction, of action on each other of bodies at a distance and not by impact. Whatever later followers of Newton may subsequently have said, this view was sternly rejected by Newton himself. By gravitation, he insisted, he meant nothing beyond the observed phenomenon, of which he offered no explanation: 'Hypotheses non fingo.' In a letter to Bentley, the Master of his College, who had been incautiously referring to a force of gravitation, Newton wrote: 'That gravity should be innate, inherent, and essential to matter, so that one body may act upon another at a distance through a *vacuum*, without the mediation of anything else, by and through which their action and force may be conveyed from one to another, is to me so great an absurdity that I believe no man who has in philosophical matters a competent faculty of thinking can ever fall into it.' A force of gravitation as an explanation of motion would, for Newton, have been just another of those occult qualities which the seventeenth-century so derided, an explanation on a par with the 'dormitive power' which Molière's medical student offered as an explanation why opium sends us to sleep. As Leibniz remarked of such alleged attractions in the Preface to *New Essay on the Human Understanding*, 'it is impossible to conceive how this takes place, i.e., to explain it mechanically'. It was acknowledged that magnetism, gravitation and the like were difficult to explain mechanically; but to explain them in terms of magnetic or gravitational forces would have been regarded as a merely verbal subterfuge.

So it was plain orthodoxy to ascribe to bodies, to atoms, those properties which mechanical science imputed to them. It was an equally unquestioned orthodoxy to deny to them all those other qualities, such as colour, taste and smell, that the common man uncritically ascribed to them. Thus Galileo, echoing the fragment of Democritus already quoted, said in *The Assayer* that 'tastes, odours, colours, and so on are no more than mere names so far as the object in which we place them is concerned, and reside only in the consciousness. Hence, if the living creature were removed, all these qualities would be wiped away and annihilated.' Bodies, Galileo claimed, cause such sensations in us by motion and impact, just as a hand may produce in us the sensation of a tickle by motion and impact; it is as absurd to locate the colour in the body as to locate the tickle in the hand that causes it. Newton expressed the same view in his magnificent prose:

If at any time I speak of light and rays as coloured or endued with colours, I would be understood to speak, not philosophically and properly, but grossly and accordingly to such conceptions as vulgar people in seeing all these experiments would be apt to frame. For the rays, to speak properly, are not coloured. In them there is nothing else than a certain power and disposition to stir up a sensation of this or that colour. For as sound in a bell or musical string, or other sounding body, is nothing but a trembling motion, and in the air nothing but that motion propagated from the object, and in the sensorium it is a sense of that motion under the form of sound, so colours in the object are nothing but a disposition to reflect this or that sort of rays more copiously than the rest; in the rays they are nothing but their dispositions to propagate this or that motion into the sensorium, and in the sensorium they are sensations of those motions under the forms of colours.

We have seen that we can find the mechanistic corpuscularian philosophy in many of the great scientists and philosophers of the seventeenth-century. But perhaps the best and clearest statement of this fundamental theory is to be found in the works of Robert Boyle, the traditional 'father of chemistry'; since it is vital for us to be well acquainted with it if we are to understand Berkeley's philosophy more than superficially, we can with advantage read Boyle's statement of it. He gives it in a monograph entitled *The Origin of Forms and Qualities* (1666), with the aim of explaining the corpuscularian philosophy to the amateur. 'Among those', he says, 'that are inclined to that philosophy, which I find I have been much imitated in calling corpuscularian, there are many ingenious persons, especially among the nobility and gentry, who . . . delight to make or see variety of experiments, without having ever had the opportunity to be instructed in the rudiments or fundamental notions of that philosophy.' So, he hopes, 'this tract may in some sort exhibit a scheme or serve for an introduction into the elements of the corpuscularian philosophy'.

Here, then, are these elements, in Boyle's own words so far as is convenient:

1 'I agree with our Epicureans in thinking that the world is made up of an innumerable multitude of singly insensible corpuscles endowed with their own sizes, shapes and motions.'

2 'If we should conceive that the rest of the universe were annihilated, except any of these entire and undivided corpuscles, it is hard to say what could be attributed to it, besides matter, motion (or rest), bulk and shape.'

3 God, Boyle holds, created the world: 'but the world being once framed, and the course of nature established, the naturalist (except in some few cases where God or incorporeal agents interpose) has recourse to the first cause but for its general support and influence, whereby it preserves matter and motion

from annihilation and destruction; and in explicating particular phenomena considers only the size, shape, motion (or want of it), texture and the resulting qualities and attributes of the small particles of matter'.

4 As for other apparent qualities of bodies, 'I have already taught that there are simpler and more primitive affections of matter, from which these secondary qualities, if I may so call them, do depend.'

5 Corpuscles strike on the sense organs and cause motions which are transmitted to the brain. 'Sensation', Boyle says, 'is properly and ultimately made in, or by, the mind or discerning faculty; which, from the differing motions of the internal parts of the brain, is excited and determined to differing perceptions to some of which men have given the name of heat, cold or other qualities.'

6 'I do not deny but that bodies may be said, in a very favourable sense, to have those qualities we call sensible, though there were no animals in the world: for a body in that case may differ from other bodies which now are quite devoid of quality in its having such a disposition of its constituent corpuscles that in case it were duly applied to the sensory of an animal, it would produce such a sensible quality which a body of another texture would not.'

The reader now has before him a sketch of the corpuscularian philosophy. He will have noticed that it was accepted by a number of eminent philosophers and scientists before the publication of John Locke's *Essay Concerning Human Understanding*, which did not appear until 1689. It is therefore rather strange that this theory is traditionally known as Locke's theory of primary and secondary qualities. Locke was, indeed, an enthusiastic disciple of Robert Boyle, whose laboratory in Oxford he visited from time to time as a young man; he was also an admiring friend of Sir Isaac Newton, and described himself as an under-labourer in the same field as those two eminent men. He gives a version, by no means original, of the corpuscularian philosophy in Book II, Chapter VIII of his *Essay*, and, since Berkeley studied this version carefully and followed its terminology, we must take notice of it, the more carefully since Locke's ambiguous language seems to have misled Berkeley into some misunderstanding of the theory. The extent to which Locke was reproducing generally accepted doctrine is well illustrated by a remark of the Rev. Henry Lee in his *Anti-Scepticism or Notes upon each Chapter of Mr Locke's Essay Concerning Human Understanding*, published in 1702. Of Locke's account of this topic he says: ''tis common to all that pretend to the Mechanical Philosophy' and that 'all this is so very clear, now so universally own'd, that this Author might have spared many of his Arguments to prove it'.

Locke lists the qualities that are 'utterly inseparable from the body' as being solidity, extension, figure, motion or rest, and number. His notion of solidity is unclear, but the most favourable interpretation of it is as the exclusive occupation of a given portion of space. These he calls primary qualities. Colour, heat, cold, taste etc. he, like the other philosophers whose views we have quoted, did not regard as being true qualities of bodies but as sensations produced in us by bodies. So he defines secondary qualities as being 'such qualities, which in truth are nothing in the objects themselves, but powers to produce various sensations in us by their primary qualities, i.e., by the bulk, figure, texture, and motion of their insensible parts, as colours, sounds, tastes, etc.'. Locke thus clearly defines secondary qualities as powers to produce sensations in us, not as being the sensations thus produced; but Locke himself occasionally, and Berkeley together with most subsequent commentators regularly, depart from this terminology and call the colours, tastes, smells etc. themselves secondary qualities.

In saying that primary qualities are utterly inseparable from bodies Locke seems to mean two things. First, these qualities are defining properties of body – whatever lacks these would not count as a body. Perhaps some bodies actually are colourless, or tasteless, or soundless, and it is at least conceivable that some are; but an unextended body, a body that was neither in motion nor at rest, a body with no shape, however irregular, would be a contradiction in terms. Secondly, nothing which has these properties can ever cease to have them, whatever be done to it, whereas a body may be deprived of its smell, its taste or its colour. So primary qualities are inseparable from bodies, while secondary qualities are not; there may be bodies which lack the power to cause our sensations of colour, smell, taste etc.

Locke, like other upholders of the corpuscularian philosophy, holds that all our sensations, whether of primary or of secondary qualities, are caused by the impact of insensible atoms on our sense organs, the motions thus generated being then transmitted by the nerves to the brain; these sensations he calls ideas. Using this terminology he claims that the ideas of primary qualities (shape, bulk, motion etc.) resemble these qualities themselves, whereas the ideas of secondary qualities do not resemble anything in the body or the powers which are the secondary qualities. Since, as I believe, Berkeley misunderstood this claim, it would be well to state it in Locke's own words: 'Ideas of primary qualities of bodies are resemblances of them, and their patterns do really exist in the bodies themselves; but the ideas produced in us by these secondary qualities have no resemblance of them at all. There is nothing like our ideas existing in the bodies themselves.'

Now when Locke says that ideas of colour and other secondary qualities do not resemble anything in the body, he does not mean that bodies are always of a colour different from that of the ideas that they produce in us; for bodies have no colour at all according to the corpuscular philosophy. He means that bodies are coloured only in the sense that they have the power to produce ideas of colour. Consistency requires that when he says that ideas of shape and of other primary qualities are resemblances of those qualities in bodies he cannot mean that bodies are always of exactly the same shape as the ideas they produce in us, that is, look to be the shape that they really are, which, in any case, is obviously false. He must mean that when we ascribe shape to bodies we do so in the same sense of 'shape' as when we ascribe it to ideas; thus 'square' when applied to either an idea or a body will have the same geometrically definable meaning. To put the point in technical jargon, ideas of primary qualities and bodies instantiate the same determinable properties – shape, size, motion etc. – but not necessarily the same determinates of those determinables on each occasion. We shall find that Berkeley attributes to Locke that interpretation of the doctrine which I have rejected; Locke does once or twice say things which give some justification for so doing; but so interpreted the doctrine is pointless and no part of the corpuscularian philosophy.

We have begun to use the terminology of ideas which was standard in the seventeenth and eighteenth centuries, and something should be said about it to conclude this introductory chapter. Descartes was the first important philosopher to use it; Locke followed him in this use and Berkeley followed Locke. So we must try to understand it now in a preliminary way, though we shall be continually faced with problems about it.

In colloquial English in the seventeenth century the word 'idea' was a synonym of 'picture', as was the word 'idée' in French. Thus Shakespeare, in *Richard III*, has Buckingham tell Gloucester that he is the 'right idea', that is, the very picture, of his father. Descartes himself said that ideas are, properly speaking, like pictures of things. The word apparently got into philosophical use in connection with a very simple theory of visual perception in which the soul sees pictures of the outside world projected on the surface of the brain, a version of the doctrine of representative perception. The term was retained even as this theory became modified or abandoned, and was also extended to cover all objects of consciousness – all sensations of all senses, the objects of memory, the objects of imagination, the objects of thought (which was often regarded as being primarily the framing of mental images), and all emotions. This widely extended use of the term 'idea' by Locke was felt to be strange and even indefensible at the time. In criticism of him Stillingfleet, then Bishop of Worcester, fulminated against 'the new way of ideas' as even dangerous to Christianity; Henry Lee, in *Anti-Scepticism*, protests that 'that only can be call'd an Idea, which is a visible Representation or Resemblance of the Object'; even well into the eighteenth-century Boswell reports Johnson as chastising current usage and pronouncing that 'it is clear that *idea* can only signify something of which an image can be formed in the mind'. It is indeed very hard to doubt that their liberal use of the word 'idea' did involve the philosophers who employed it in ambiguity and obscurity, as we shall find in our study of Berkeley's philosophy.

The philosophers of this period, like many philosophers at all other times, were quite convinced that in perception what they were aware of was an idea, an image, a sensation, caused by inherently imperceptible matter. The reader may well wonder why they were so sure that such a causal theory was true and that the 'vulgar' notion that we are immediately aware of physical objects was not worthy of serious philosophical debate. They were moved by two basic considerations. The first was that an accurate account of what we perceive, that is, of how things look to us, will be different from an accurate account of how the world is, even as it is popularly conceived to be. Thus the stick in the water is straight, but the 'stick' we perceive is bent and has no physical reality; the railway lines are parallel, but we see two lines converging in the distance; the medium dry table wine will taste sweet after we have drunk very dry sherry and dry after we have drunk a cream sherry. If the descriptions of the world and of what we perceive are thus different, what we perceive cannot be the world.

A second consideration weighed just as heavily. If the scientific account of physical reality and of the complex physical and physiological processes involved in perception is even approximately true, it is impossible to claim that we perceive such a world immediately and directly; if, for example, sound is physical vibrations in the atmosphere and is transmitted to us via motions in the ear, the nerves and the brain, then what we hear will not be physical sound, for what we hear is not a motion nor anything else mentioned in a physical account of sound.

Whether these arguments are satisfactory we must inquire later on, but not yet. But they certainly convinced the philosophers whom we have been discussing, and though Berkeley could not make use of the second of the two arguments just presented, he certainly accepted without any serious debate the conclusion that what we are aware of is ideas.

2 The attack on matter

George Berkeley was born on 12 March 1685, near Kilkenny in Ireland. His ancestry was English, but his grandfather, a royalist, moved to Ireland at the time of the restoration. Berkeley considered himself to be an Irishman; he referred to Newton as 'a philosopher of a neighbouring nation' (P 110) and, commenting sarcastically in his private notebook on what he regarded as a philosophical absurdity, he wrote: 'We Irishmen cannot attain to these truths' (C 392). He was sent to Kilkenny College, which Congreve and Swift had recently attended, and then, aged only fifteen, to Trinity College, Dublin, in 1700. There he studied mathematics, languages, including Latin, Greek, French and Hebrew, logic and philosophy; the philosophy course was up to date and included the study of Locke, the French philosopher-theologian Malebranche, and other very recent and contemporary thinkers. He graduated B.A. in 1704 at the age of nineteen and then remained at Trinity College studying privately until he was elected to a fellowship in 1707. He was ordained deacon in 1709 and priest in 1710; he continued to hold his fellowship until 1724, when he resigned to become Dean of Derry, though extended leaves of absence took him first to London and then to Italy.

Though he continued to write for many years after leaving Trinity College, Dublin, it was during the tenure of his fellowship that he wrote the works for which he is now famous. His first work, *An Essay towards a New Theory of Vision*, appeared in 1709, when he was twenty-four; it is a work as much of experimental psychology as of philosophy, and in it he principally discusses how we perceive by sight the distance, size and position of objects. The next year, in 1710, he published *A Treatise concerning the Principles of Human Knowledge*, usually known simply as *The Principles*; this is the most important of all Berkeley's writings and contains the most complete account we have of the philosophical position which he was never to abandon. In 1713 he published the *Three Dialogues between*

Hylas and Philonous, a more popular exposition of his view in which Philonous (whose name means 'lover of mind') vanquishes in argument and converts to his view Hylas ('matter'), the materialist. In 1712 he published his Latin essay *De motu* [*On Motion*] which contains by far the fullest account we have of Berkeley's view of the nature of the natural sciences.

Those are the main works published by Berkeley from which we may learn his basic metaphysical and epistemological doctrines, bearing witness to a youth of extraordinary intellectual activity. But, in addition to his published writings, we also have available to us a unique and most interesting document. In 1705, soon after graduating, Berkeley started to write a series of notes on philosophical topics in which he worked out the basis of his new and revolutionary views and made strategic plans for their publication. These notes contain ideas which he immediately rejects and theories which are silently abandoned in his published works, as well as the essential of his position; one cannot therefore safely attribute to him views found only there and not in the published work. But these notes are most valuable as an aid to the correct understanding of the published works and shed fascinating light on the creative processes of a philosopher of genius. They were written in a quarto notebook which was unknown until it was discovered by A. C. Fraser and published by him in 1871 under the title *Commonplace Book*; later editors disliked this name and the notes are now generally called *The Philosophical Commentaries*.

Berkeley's main targets for attack were to be John Locke and Sir Isaac Newton; he was well acquainted with the works of both and admired both of them greatly. Of Newton he wrote: 'I have taken as much pains as (I sincerely believe) any man living to understand that great author, and to make sense of his principles ... So that, if I do not understand him, it is not my fault but my misfortune' (L iv 116). He also referred to Newton as 'a philosopher of a neighbouring nation whom all the world admire' (P 110), and as 'an extraordinary mathematician, a profound naturalist, a person of the greatest abilities and erudition' (L iv 114). Of Locke he wrote in his notebook: 'Wonderful in Locke that he could, when advanced in years, see at all thro' a mist; it had been so long agathering and was consequently thick. This more to be admired than that he did not see farther' (C 567). He is, of course, using the word 'admire' in its usual sense at that time of 'wonder at'.

But this respect was not extended to all those whom Berkeley called the mathematicians; in his private notebook he wrote: 'I see no wit in any of them but Newton. The rest are mere triflers, mere Nihilarians' (C 372). But these words were for his eyes only; he realised that in a publication, as a young man attacking the establishment, he must exhibit a more conciliatory attitude. So in the same notebook he wrote: 'Mem. Upon all occasions to use the utmost modesty – to confute the mathematicians with the utmost civility and respect, not to style them Nihilarians, etc. N.B. To rein in ye satirical nature' (C 633–4). There are many self-addressed memoranda in the notebooks, often significant, often amusing, and only rarely opaque like: 'Mem. Story of Mr. Deering's aunt' (C 201).

So the principal objects of attack were Newton and Locke. But there was only one main element in their views that he repudiated, that being the doctrine of matter. Berkeley shared their view that ideas are the sole object of the human mind, for example. It is most vital to remember the historical context in which he was writing; often the modern reader finds Berkeley assuming, without more than perfunctory argument at most, things which to him are obscure and doubtful; these are generally things that at the time were accepted by most men and certainly by his opponents, who would have found it tedious and uncalled-for if he had argued them at length. It is also important to be aware that Berkeley never questioned the value of Newton's scientific work, which he believed to be independent of the doctrine of matter. But this doctrine he regarded as an unintelligible and totally superfluous element in his views and one that could be excised without damage to what was left. He attacked it because he believed that it was false, and he attacked it with passion because he believed that it had evil practical consequences. The full title of the *Principles*, the work in which he first attacked the doctrine of matter, is significant: *A Treatise concerning the Principles of Human Knowledge wherein the chief causes of error and difficulty in the sciences, with the grounds of scepticism, atheism, and irreligion, are inquired into.*

So there are at present four main tasks before us: first, to understand why Berkeley thought matter unintelligible; second, to understand why he thought matter superfluous; thirdly, to discover why he thought belief in it dangerous; fourth, to see what account of the world Berkeley was able to give without incorporating matter into it.

The unintelligibility of matter

To understand why Berkeley thought that matter was unintelligible, that the word 'matter' was without meaning in the way it was used by Newton and Locke, we must first realise that he was in a certain respect an extreme empiricist. The concept of empiricism is itself vague, and different philosophers have understood it differently; but luckily we need not go into this problem, for the way in which Berkeley was an empiricist becomes clear from the very first sentence of the *Principles of Human Knowledge*. This sentence reads as follows:

> It is evident to any one who takes a survey of the *objects of human knowledge*, that they are either *ideas* actually imprinted on the senses; or else such as are perceived by attending to the passions and operations of the mind; or lastly, *ideas* formed by help of memory and imagination – either compounding, dividing, or barely representing those originally perceived in the aforesaid ways.

By ideas imprinted on the senses he means visual images, heat, smells, tastes and all what Locke would have called ideas of primary and secondary qualities; ideas obtained by attending to the passions include introspective awareness of love, hatred, joy, grief and the like – we can think of these passions because we have experienced them. By attending to the operations of the mind we acquire the ideas of thought itself, of memory, of imagination, and so forth. The ideas gained in these various ways can be recalled in the memory, and in the imagination we can compound and divide to produce what are in some sense new ideas – we can imagine a dragon or a mermaid. But this *is* composition and division; we divide our ideas of the human body and the body of a fish, and by compounding the top end of a human body and the lower end of a fishy body we make the idea or mental picture of a mermaid. So all the materials of thought are such as are supplied by experience, and we cannot think about or have knowledge about what is not the kind of thing we have experienced.

This empiricism is much emphasised in Berkeley's private notebooks: 'Foolish in men to despise the senses. If it were not for them the mind could have no knowledge, no thought at all'; 'By *idea* I mean any sensible or imaginable thing'; 'Pure intellect I understand not' (C 539, 775, 810). He even sets out his empiricism in five simple propositions:

1 All significant words stand for ideas.
2 All knowledge about our ideas.
3 All ideas come from without or from within.
4 If from without it must be by the senses, and they are called sensations.
5 If from within they are the operations of the mind, and are called thoughts. (C 378)

Some philosophers of the seventeenth and eighteenth centuries had rejected empiricism of this kind. Thus Descartes and Leibniz claimed that since they had the idea of God, the idea of matter, the idea of soul or spirit, and since these were not obtainable in experience, there must, therefore, be what they called innate ideas, ideas which the human mind was so constituted as to frame and apply to experience without gaining them in experience. Such ideas were not sensible or picture-like. Since Locke had repudiated any such view, Berkeley did not think it necessary to argue against it; as the opening words of the *Principles*, quoted above, make clear, he himself thought it was evidently wrong. Locke, on the other hand, in spite of having expressly argued against innate ideas, still claimed to have the ideas of God, of substance, of matter and the like. This Berkeley attributed to Locke's recognition of a class of abstract ideas. In addition to the mind's compounding and dividing of ideas, which Berkeley allowed, Locke attributed to the mind a further power of forming ideas by abstraction, and it was this that Berkeley thought to be the cause of what he regarded as Locke's mistake. As for Berkeley, since he was an extreme empiricist he denied that he had any idea of an inherently imperceptible matter, an imperceptible God or even of imperceptible 'finite spirits'; just how Berkeley managed to combine this empiricism with his undoubted and undoubting Christian orthodoxy we shall obviously have to inquire in due course.

Let us try to understand the basic grounds for the rejection of matter as unintelligible a little more fully before we examine the detail of Berkeley's arguments, which vary greatly in cogency. It is clear that, for Berkeley, what we can think of must be imaginable; for all objects of the mind are ideas and by an idea Berkeley means what is sensible or imaginable, and what is sensible is imaginable. But matter is said by its adherents to be something which is not coloured, not warm or tepid or cold, odourless, tasteless etc. – the ideas of secondary qualities resemble nothing in matter. So if we try to imagine matter it is impossible, since we cannot imagine anything that lacks all secondary qualities. If I visualise something it must have some colour, however dingy and nondescript; it cannot just be a shape of no colour at all if I am to see it. If I imagine myself touching something it must feel hard or soft, and clearly the senses of hearing, taste and smell are concerned exclusively with secondary qualities. So one cannot perceive something having only primary qualities, nor can one imagine such a thing; yet that is what matter is supposed to be. So one cannot have an idea of matter, it cannot be an object of one's mind, it is unthinkable; we can attach no meaning to the word 'matter'. Perhaps at this stage of the argument some will be inclined to protest that though we cannot *imagine* matter as defined by Newton and Locke we can *conceive* of it in abstraction from secondary qualities. But Berkeley is prepared for this move; it involves, he thinks, Locke's doctrine of abstract ideas, and this, he believes, he can show to be absurd.

But let us not yet pursue the details of Berkeley's argument. First we should see that the line he takes is quite persuasive, independently of the particular form in which he presents it. Three-quarters of a century later, Kant will attack Berkeley's presentation of the argument as he understands it; but he too will argue that concepts can be applied only to phenomena and not to things in themselves, that we can think only about objects of possible experience, which certainly do not include matter. In the present century many have argued that of statements that purport to describe the world those alone were meaningful which were capable of verification and falsification by empirical means; but statements to the effect that what we experience is caused by an imperceptible matter are certainly unverifiable experimentally.

The argument may be put, as it was sometimes put by Berkeley, in a linguistic form. If we ask how we can come to understand, say, the word 'red', it would seem that, in principle, it can only be by somebody pointing to something red and saying 'That is red' – in principle, since clearly we learn such words by a less formal version of the same process; perhaps we hear somebody say to somebody else 'I do hate that shocking pink dress that that girl is wearing', we take a look at the dress, and say to ourselves 'So that is shocking pink, is it?' If one were ignorant of the game of rugby football, one could learn the meaning of the word 'scrum' by observing in what circumstances it is proper to say such things as 'A scrum has been formed' and so on. Of course, it is much more likely that we shall learn the meaning of such words at least partly by verbal explanation; but to verbal explanation an end must come. Some basic stock of words, it seems clear, must be learnt by confrontation with experience, before verbal explanation can begin.

But language can be abused. In Berkeley's own words, 'there are many names in use among speculative men which do not always suggest to others determinate, particular ideas, or in truth anything at all' (P, introduction, para. 19). The abuse may be conscious and in jest, as when a modern philosopher, being teased for requiring more sleep than most people, replied that she did not sleep more than other people, she simply slept more slowly. It may be hard to determine whether a use of words is an abuse; thus Newton spoke of absolute motion and contrasted it with relative motion; Berkeley in the *Principles* claimed that this was an abuse of words and that no meaning could be attached to the expression 'absolute motion'. Most scientists and philosophers since have followed Berkeley in this, but what Newton could not see could not be *obviously* right. But it is very hard to doubt that in some abstract disciplines, such as philosophy, meaning can become so rarified as to be undetectable.

It is clear that the word 'matter' has uses in which it is readily intelligible. As Berkeley represents Philonous as saying in the *Dialogues*: 'If by *material substance* is meant only *sensible body* . . . then I am more certain of matter's existence than you or any other philosopher pretend to be' (L ii 237). But the argument is that if matter is to be regarded as something inherently imperceptible then 'the Matter philosophers contend for is an incomprehensible Somewhat' (L ii 233). The word is familiar and so we overlook the fact that we have attenuated its meaning until it has vanished into thin air.

There is another argument that Berkeley uses against the intelligibility of matter which is rather more obviously unsatisfactory and rests on a confusion between the notions of substance and of matter. In this argument Berkeley very significantly refers to material substance rather than simply to matter. The essentials of this argument can readily be given in Berkeley's own words.

> If we inquire into what the most accurate philosophers declare themselves to mean by *material substance*, we shall find them acknowledge they have no other meaning annexed to those sounds but the idea of Being in general, together with the relative notion of its supporting accidents. The general idea of Being appeareth to me the most abstract and incomprehensible of all other [, while] it is evident *support* cannot here be taken in its usual or literal sense, as when we say that pillars support a building. In what sense therefore must it be taken? For my part I am not able to discover any sense at all that can be applicable to it. (P 17)

In referring to 'the most accurate philosophers' Berkeley clearly has in mind principally John Locke and, indeed, the following passage from Locke's *Essay on Human Understanding*: 'If any one will examine himself concerning his notion of pure substance in general, he will find he has no other idea of it at all, but only a supposition of he knows not what support of such qualities which are capable of producing simple ideas in us.' But this is an admission, or, rather, a claim, that the notion of substance is ultimately unintelligible, not an admission that the notion of matter is in any way defective. Locke sees the same difficulty in the notion of substance whether we are talking about bodily or mental substances, as the following quotation shows: 'we have as clear a notion of the substance of spirit as we have of body: the one being supposed to be (without knowing what it is) the *substratum* to those simple ideas we have from without; and the other supposed (with a like ignorance of what it is) to be the *substratum* to those operations which we experiment in ourselves within'.

It is surely clear that the dubious intelligibility of the notion of substance as the mere somewhat that is the bearer of the qualities attributed to it cannot be properly taken to throw doubt on the concept of matter. Matter is not an indescribable somewhat supporting qualities but an imperceptible cause of perceptible ideas; both these views may be unacceptable, but, if so, the unacceptability of matter cannot be derived from the unacceptability of substance. The doctrine of matter is independent of the substance–attribute analysis of things, which appears only in Locke among the authorities we have quoted. By speaking of material substance so often Berkeley allows himself to confuse two distinct issues.

The superfluity of matter

We have seen Berkeley's reasons for wishing to maintain that the corpuscularian philosophers had been unsuccessful in their attempts to make their concept of an inherently imperceptible matter intelligible. It might have been the case that if matter were rejected a gap would be left and it would be necessary to postulate something else to fill the gap thus left. But Berkeley thought that this was not so; not only was matter unintelligible, but there was no gap to be filled: a complete and satisfying account of the world could be given without invoking it or any substitute for it.

If we look at Locke's inventory of the furniture of the world it would seem to include four elements:

1 God, the creator of everything else and the law-maker who determines the character and history of his creation.

2 Matter, which for certain purposes we may divide into that

which impinges on our sense-organs to cause ideas and that which constitutes the sense-organs and nervous system on which other matter acts. But there is here no fundamental difference.

3 Ideas, which are mental but caused by the action of matter on the nervous system.

4 The mind that is aware of these ideas and operates on them and with them in thinking.

This ontology, which was shared in all essentials by Newton, most conspicuously lacks the physical object of common, everyday thought and discourse. We can, of course, still speak of chairs and tables; but on the physical side they are but dense collections of elementary corpuscles, and our seeing a chair or table is merely the occurrence of certain ideas caused by the particles emitted by such a collection. A further point to be noted is that the causal links between the elements in Locke's ontology are inexplicable. That the actions and purposes of God are inscrutable we may take for granted; but also the way in which matter acts on mind to produce ideas is scientifically inexplicable. A causal story in mechanistic terms can be given of particles being emitted from those collections of particles which constitute physical bodies; these particles strike on the eye or other sense-organs and by impact on the nerve-endings cause motion in the 'animal spirits' which were conjectured to be contained in the nerves; the motions of the animal spirits in the nerves is itself communicated to the brain; but how the motions of the particles that constitute the relevant portion of the brain cause the occurrence of ideas in the mind is not mechanically explicable (and perhaps modern physiology is equally powerless to offer an explanation). Locke gives an example: 'a violet, by the impulse of such insensible particles of matter of peculiar figures and bulks, and in different degrees and modifications of their motions, causes the ideas of the blue colour and sweet scent of that flower to be produced in our minds; it being no more impossible to conceive that God should annex such ideas to such motions with which they have no similitude, than that he should annex the idea of pain to the motion of a piece of steel dividing our flesh'. So Locke has to appeal to the direct action of God, without any scientific explanation of how the links in the causal chain are joined together.

If we look to see what reasons Locke had to offer for his belief in matter, we are bound to be disappointed. In the chapter entitled 'Of our knowledge of the existence of other things' in Book IV of his *Essay* he tells us that it can be gained only by sensation; but it is far from clear how knowledge of the existence of imperceptible matter could thus be gained. He tells us that our certainty is as great as our condition needs and, assuming that unless we posit matter we must consider waking to be indistinguishable from dreaming, tells the doubter that he 'doth but dream that he makes the question; and so it is not much matter that a waking man should answer him'. But knockabout humour is scarcely an adequate substitute for argument on such topics as these.

But Locke also says that 'it is plain those perceptions are produced in us by exterior causes affecting our senses', and it is this that Berkeley assumes to be the main argument that leads to a belief in matter. God, on this view, created matter to be the causal agency through which ideas are caused in sentient creatures. Thus, in the dialogues between Hylas and Philonous, when Hylas is driven to admit that he cannot sustain the notion of matter as conceived of by Locke and Newton, he falls back on the claim that matter is 'an instrument, subservient to the supreme Agent in the production of our ideas', and argues that he has some understanding of matter since 'I have some notion of *instrument in general*', which I apply to it.'

To this move Berkeley has a blistering retort, the essence of which can be given in the words given by Berkeley to Philonous:

'Is it not common to all instruments, that they are applied to the doing those things only which cannot be performed by the mere act of our wills? . . . How therefore can you suppose that an All-perfect Spirit, on whose Will all things have an absolute and immediate dependence, should need an instrument in his operation, or, not needing it, make use of it? . . . And the use of an instrument sheweth the agent to be limited by rules of another's prescription, and that he cannot obtain his end but in such a way, and by such conditions. Whence it seems a clear consequence, that the supreme unlimited Agent useth no tool or instrument at all.' (L ii 218–19)

This argument, of course, assumes that there is a God who is the omnipotent first cause; but, since those he was arguing against conceded it, Berkeley was entitled to make the assumption when arguing against them, especially as he had arguments for the existence of God in reserve. Given this basic assumption, the argument seems good. To postulate both God and matter as an explanation of our sense-experience seems to be superfluous, especially when it is agreed to be totally obscure why the hypothetical matter should cause sensations of the character that they do in fact have. Thus Berkeley at this point seems justified in claiming that the ontology of Locke is redundant and matter is superfluous. In the next two chapters we shall examine Berkeley's positive acccounts of science and common sense without the aid of the concept of matter; but first we must consider one more attack on the materialists to which Berkeley attached great importance.

Abstract ideas

We have seen that it is basic to Berkeley's attack on matter to hold that to think of something is, ultimately, to imagine it. Matter is unintelligible precisely because one could not see or imagine anything of the kind that matter is supposed to be, having primary qualities but lacking colour, smell, taste or sound. Berkeley is aware that at this stage some of his opponents, then as in our day, will want to claim that Berkeley's criteria of intelligibility are too restrictive. In the jargon of the philosophy of Berkeley's time the objection takes the form that while matter is not imaginable we can none the less have an abstract idea of matter. This Berkeley denies. Before we can consider the controversy we must try to understand the theory of abstract ideas, and this will be the objective of the next few pages.

It was a rarely questioned orthodoxy among the principal philosophers of the seventeenth and eighteenth centuries that thinking was primarily having ideas before the mind. That one can think in words was, of course, recognised, but language was regarded as being actually necessary only for purposes of communication with others. In Locke's typical words: 'The comfort and advantage of society not being to be had without communication of thoughts, it was necessary that man should find out some external sensible signs, whereby those invisible ideas which his thoughts are made up of might be made known to others.' One could think privately in words; but words stood to ideas as cheques do to real money, and cheques could be returned to drawer. All agreed that thinking in words could be dangerous – 'Words often used without signification' is one of Locke's section headings.

With this view of the relation between thinking in ideas and thinking in words, which can indeed be traced back to Aristotle's *On Interpretation*, Berkeley was in full agreement. Moreover, he was convinced that most of the unintelligible metaphysics that he was attacking resulted from bogus thinking in meaningless words; the last eight paragraphs of his introduction to the *Principles* are devoted to explaining that this is so. In paragraph 21 of this introduction he writes:

> Most parts of knowledge have been so strangely perplexed and darkened by the abuse of words, and general ways of speech wherein they are delivered, that it may almost be made a question whether language has contributed more to the hindrance or advancement of the sciences. Since words are so apt to impose on the understanding, I am resolved in my inquiries to make as little use of them as possibly I can: whatever ideas I consider, I shall endeavour to take them bare and naked into my view; keeping out of my thoughts, so far as I am able, those names which long and constant use hath so strictly united with them.

But what is it to think in bare and naked ideas? It is clear that basically ideas were thought of as mental images, and 'image' or 'picture' was the normal seventeenth-century meaning of 'idea' in non-philosophical writing also. Even the rationalistic Descartes, who was mainly responsible for the wide currency of the word 'idea' in philosophy, said that 'some of our thoughts are like pictures of things, to which alone the name idea is properly suited'. Both Berkeley and Hume clearly regard thinking in ideas to consist in having mental images, and for Locke too, at least when alleged abstract ideas are not involved, it seems that ideas are normally mental images; he can speak of 'ideas or images' as if the terms were interchangeable.

But it is not clear what thinking in mental images is supposed to be. Just having a mental image does not seem to be enough. One may, for example, have a mental image which is approximately round and red, but this on its own scarcely seems to be a thought about anything. Let us suppose that this red and round image has a close resemblance to a tomato, since there is no doubt that the philosophers with whom we are concerned believed that resemblance made the idea an appropriate way of thinking about some object. But if the occurrence of the idea is a thought, and indeed a thought having some reference to tomatoes, it remains unclear what thought about tomatoes it is. Let us make a list of possible candidates, expressed in verbal form:

This is a tomato; Tomatoes are red; That tomato was red and round; Some tomatoes are red; The tomato is a fruit; Is this a tomato? Some round objects are red.

Which, if any, of these, and of countless other possible candidates, is the appropriate verbalisation of the thought one thinks when one has before one's mind the round, red image resembling a tomato?

The difficulty can be approached from the opposite direction. Let us suppose that one is to have the thought 'This is white' in the form of an idea or mental image. Now if we summon up a white mental image it cannot be just white and have no other characteristics; it must presumably be bright or drab, round or of some other shape, with this or that background. Let us suppose that it is bright and round as well as white, and now the problem is what determines that the occurrence of the idea constitutes the thought 'This is white' rather than the thought 'This is bright' or 'This is round', if, indeed, it constitutes any of them.

These difficulties were to some extent seen, though not with exemplary clarity, by Locke among others. He, relying heavily on *The Art of Thinking* by Descartes' friend and collaborator, the theologian Arnauld (1612–94), made use of the notion of abstract ideas to try to solve some of them. Most of our thinking requires abstract ideas, according to Locke. He holds that of the words of the English language only proper names signify concrete or particular ideas; all other words which stand for any idea at all stand for abstract ideas. So abstract ideas are as essential to non-verbal thought as words other than proper names are essential to its verbal expression.

What then is an abstract idea? Locke tells us four times in his *Essay*, in Book II, Chapter xi, Section 9, Book II, Chapter xii, Section 1, Book III, Chapter iii, Sections 6 and 10 and Book IV, Chapter vii, Section 9. Of these the first three are very similar to each other; since Berkeley in his violent attack on abstract ideas quotes only the final and most paradoxical account from Book IV, we should perhaps note what these other concurring accounts say. In Book II Chapter xi we read:

> The mind makes the particular *ideas*, received from particular objects, to become general; which is done by considering them as they are in the mind such appearances, separate from all other existences, and the circumstances of real existence, as time, place, or any other, concomitant *ideas*. This is called ABSTRACTION, whereby *ideas* taken from particular beings become general representatives of all of the same kind; and their names general names, applicable to whatever exists conformable to such abstract *ideas*. Such precise, naked appearances in the mind, without considering how, whence, or with what others they came there, the understanding lays up (with names commonly annexed to them) as the standards to rank real existence into sorts, as they agree with these patterns, and to *denominate* them accordingly. Thus the same colour being observed today in chalk or snow, which the mind yesterday received from milk, it considers that appearance alone, makes it a representative of all of that kind; and having given it the name *whiteness*, it by that sound signifies the same quality wheresoever to be imagined or met with; and thus universals, whether *ideas* or terms, are made.

This is not entirely unambiguous, for it is not clear what considering whiteness separately involves. If it is simply a matter of disregarding all other features of the idea, then a white, bright and round image can be used as the abstract idea of white by simply ignoring the other features and treating it as the general representative of everything having this feature. Similarly the same image could have been made the abstract idea of brightness, if we had chosen to disregard the whiteness and other features. Presumably it could have been made the general idea of colour by disregarding the differences between it and red or green images. While this is by no means a full and adequate explanation, we do have here some indication of how having a red and round mental image could constitute the occurrence of a thought and of one particular thought rather than another. In principle, the answer is that it becomes such as a result of some rule-like decision; a red and round image may become the thought of a tomato if we decide to treat this image as the general representative of all things having the characteristics of a tomato.

But there is another possible interpretation of Locke's words, in which the word 'separate' is taken more literally. On this interpretation, when Locke speaks of separating the colour of milk from all other circumstances and ideas he is demanding that we should have an image of which the only possible description is that it is white. On this interpretation it would seem that he is demanding the evidently impossible and, since it is better to interpret an author as making sense when it is possible plausibly to do so, we may well prefer the first interpretation.

Berkeley, however, quotes only the perplexing words of Book IV of Locke's *Essay*, in which the following extract occurs:

> Does it not require some pains and skill to form the *general idea* of a *triangle* (which is yet none of the most abstract . . .), for it must be neither oblique nor rectangle, neither equilateral, equicrural, nor scalenon; but all and none of these at once. In effect, it is something imperfect that cannot exist, an *idea* wherein some parts of several different and inconsistent ideas are put together.

Berkeley has a good deal of fun from this. In his notebooks he had written: 'Mem. To bring the killing blow at the last, e.g. in the matter of abstraction to bring Locke's general triangle in the last' (C 687). He refers to it sarcastically as sublime speculations. It seemed to him to be self-evidently absurd.

But, once again, it is possible to interpret Locke here as making better sense, regarding the literal absurdities in his account as rhetoric in a purple passage glorifying the rational powers of mankind. If we ask whether the concept of a triangle includes being isosceles or scalene, the answer is that it includes neither, since it is possible to deny either of them of some triangles; in this sense the abstract idea of *triangle* is of something neither scalene nor isosceles. If we ask whether the concept of a triangle excludes being isosceles or scalene, the answer is that it excludes neither, since it is possible to assert either of them of some triangles; in this sense the abstract idea of triangle includes both being isosceles and being scalene. But since nothing can be merely triangular without being either equilateral, scalene or isosceles, being *triangular* cannot be a complete account of any existent thing. Thus Locke's rhetoric may be taken as illustrating the character of a generic concept which covers several species, though it must be owned that his wording invites misunderstanding if I have correctly interpreted him.

Rightly or wrongly, however, Berkeley regards the doctrine of abstract ideas as requiring there to be mental image of an essentially indeterminate nature, and this he regards as absurd. Even if there is the possibility of some degree of indeterminacy of images (if we imagine a speckled hen must it have some definite number of speckles?), still the notion of an image which is merely, say, white and nothing else is indeed absurd, and Berkeley is surely right in rejecting the doctrine of abstract ideas as he interprets it.

Given this view of the theory of abstract ideas, two points now need to be discussed. First, why does Berkeley think that the theory aids and promotes the metaphysics of materialism; secondly, what account does Berkeley give of thinking non-verbally without the aid of abstract ideas?

It is basic to Berkeley's position to claim that matter as described verbally by the corpuscularians is unintelligible since we cannot imagine anything which has primary qualities but including no ideas of secondary qualities. We cannot, for example, visualise a colourless expanse. He also thinks that, while some would claim to think of unperceived objects, it is obviously impossible to imagine an unperceived object, to separate existence from being perceived. What Berkeley is doing in his attack on abstract ideas is to counter the move that, while matter is not imaginable, it is none the less conceivable, since we can have an abstract idea of extension without colour, just as we can have, as Locke explained, an abstract idea of whiteness. In the same way, says Berkeley's imaginary opponent, we can conceive of an object existing unperceived, since we can abstract existence from perception and imagination.

Given Berkeley's interpretation of abstract ideas, which surely does make them indefensible, it is clear that he is right in thinking that the intelligibility of matter cannot be defended by an appeal to them. What I find odd is the claim of Berkeley that the doctrine of abstract ideas was closely connected with the belief in matter. I can think of no place where Locke or any other philosopher made use of the doctrine of abstract ideas to defend the intelligibility of matter. Moreover, if the alternative account of this doctrine which I have put forward is correct, the doctrine could not be used in this way. As I understand Locke, he is explaining not how whiteness, for example, can be conceived of as existing on its own, but how we can think of whiteness as distinct from the other features that any white thing would have; so the fact that we can think of the primary qualities without thinking of colour or taste could not be consistently regarded by Locke as a ground for believing in the existence of colourless and tasteless matter. It is not clear that Locke ever saw the problem of the intelligibility of matter on an empiricist hypothesis, or *a fortiori*, that he ever defended it. It was one of Berkeley's achievements to see the problem.

So Berkeley will have no truck with abstract ideas. But he does recognise that he must give some account of generality. If, as Berkeley seems to think, we can give an adequate account of thinking of a triangle – some particular triangle – in terms of having an image of it, what account is he to give of the thought of all triangles? He starts to do this in the introduction to the *Principles* by making a distinction between a special kind of idea, called an abstract idea, which cannot exist, and a general idea which is not a special kind of idea, but simply an ordinary idea or mental image that fulfils a special function. Generality, he holds, is a kind of role, not an internal characteristic. An idea is made general 'by being made to represent or stand for all particular ideas of the same sort' (para. 12). He illustrates his meaning with an example drawn from geometry. A geometer will prove some theorem with reference to some particular line; but the proof is general because, though it is one particular line, 'as it is there used, it represents all particular lines whatever', and Berkeley takes this proof to be the same as one concerning 'a line in general'. General ideas are on a par with the drawn line of the geometer.

Berkeley is surely right in claiming that a sign becomes general not by acquiring a peculiar character but by being used in a certain way. A full discussion is impossible here, but one or two difficulties may be mentioned. First, Berkeley says, in a quotation given in our previous paragraph, that the general idea is to represent all particular ideas 'of the same sort'. But, if I have before my mind some particular idea of, say, a line, how am I to know whether it is representative of all lines or of all short lines, or of all straight lines, or of all geometrical figures, or . . .? If it is to be representative of all *lines*, do I perhaps need to have the general idea of a line already to determine what is of the same sort and so what the line represents? But this clearly leads to a vicious regress.

The second difficulty is one which beset all the theorists who used the terminology of ideas. If we consider verbal thought we can readily distinguish between the words we use, which we may call the thought-vehicle, and the object of thought. If I think 'The cat is on the mat', the thought-vehicle is that set of five words, and the object of thought an animal. I can, of course, think about words in words, as when I think of 'The cat is on the mat' that it contains five words. But still the words which are the thought-vehicle are readily distinguished from the words which are the object of thought. Now if we regard the objects of our experience as being really ideas and not cats and mats, and if we call thinking the having of ideas, then we call the thought-vehicle and all objects of thought by the same name, 'idea'. Confusion can easily result, and historically it did.

Will an image in the mind of Berkeley's geometer, working 'in his head', be a thought-vehicle or the object of thought? Will the line be the non-verbal equivalent of the word 'line'? But the proof in words is not about the word 'line', and so the proof in non-verbal form should not be about the non-verbal equivalent of the word; *a fortiori*, the proof in neither case should be about it and everything of the same sort. We have got to distinguish between a line used as an iconic symbol to represent lines and one of the representative lines which it iconically represents. The word 'represent' is surely, as illustrated here, dangerously ambiguous in Berkeley's account.

So this chapter must end with two questions. First, does Berkeley succeed in giving an adequate alternative to Locke's account of general ideas in terms of abstraction? Secondly, if we take the alternative interpretation of Locke's theory which was suggested earlier in this discussion, does it not conform to Berkeley's requirement that generality be a question of function rather than of its internal character? Perhaps it is what Berkeley needs, when it is so interpreted. But generality is a very difficult subject which intensive modern study has still left full of difficulties. Nobody in the time of Locke and Berkeley had the conceptual apparatus to give an adequate account of it.

3 Immaterialism and common sense

So Berkeley has claimed that matter is unintelligible. We cannot imagine anything like it any more than we can observe it, and the invocation of abstract ideas by means of which we may think of the unimaginable involves absurdity. In so far as we allow matter to be vaguely intelligible as a tool or instrument of God we can see that, thought of as such a tool, it is superfluous: 'to what end should God take these roundabout methods of effecting things by instruments and machines, which no one can deny might have been effected by the mere command of His will, without all that apparatus?' (P 61). Moreover, even those who, like Locke, postulate the existence of matter acknowledge that they cannot explain the character of our experience by reference to matter; physics cannot explain why certain pulsations of the air cause heard sound or why in certain physical conditions we see one colour rather than another, or, indeed, why we see any colour at all. The most that Locke can plead is that it is 'no more impossible to conceive that God should annex such ideas to such motions with which they have no similitude, than that he should annex the idea of pain to the motion of a piece of steel dividing our flesh'; but, says Berkeley 'how Matter should operate on a Spirit, or procure any idea in it, is what no philosopher will pretend to explain' (P 50). Berkeley also wished to claim that the only causal agency that was intelligible was of the kind we know in acting ourselves, as when we summon up one idea or another; all we witness in the physical world is succession, regular or irregular, so that the causal agency of matter was yet another unintelligible postulate.

So on all counts it seemed clear to Berkeley that in the ontology of Locke, Newton and their associates matter was indefensible and superfluous. They themselves were ready to admit that matter without God yielded no satisfactory explanation of the world. So Berkeley claims that a complete account of the world can be given in terms of the remainder of the Newtonian ontology – God, finite spirits and their ideas. In a famous formulation of this doctrine Berkeley said that to exist is either to perceive (*percipere*), which consitutes the existence of spirits, or to be perceived (*percipi*), which constitutes the existence of the inanimate, of ideas. These perceived ideas are objects of the mind which have no existence independent of the mind. So the world is ultimately spiritual; there is nothing beyond minds and their contents.

At least at first sight, this is an outrageous doctrine, one which is incompatible not only with the presuppositions of science but also with common sense. It seems to deny the existence both of the matter which the physical sciences investigate and of the familiar objects of the everyday world, the chairs and tables, the mountains, plains and rivers which surround us and which we all believe to exist independently of ourselves. It is manifestly contrary to common sense to say that bodies do not exist when we do not observe them.

Berkeley was prepared to agree that if his views were incompatible with common sense and made science impossible they would be unacceptable. What makes his philosophy interesting is that he claims that his ontology is perfectly compatible with both common sense and religious beliefs and that, while it admittedly contradicts a metaphysical presupposition of the scientists, he can give a satisfactory account of the nature and value of the sciences without invoking the hypothesis of matter. Moreover, he develops this claim with such ingenuity that it has always been notoriously difficult to refute him.

We shall start by expounding in this chapter Berkeley's arguments designed to show that he can on his basis account for all that common sense requires. In the next chapter we shall look to see what account he can give of the nature of science on his immaterialist hypothesis. Finally we shall consider what account he can give of God and of finite spirits. Since this topic is being so long postponed for full treatment one or two preliminary words on it are perhaps desirable now. One of the first objections to Berkeley which are likely to occur to his readers is that if matter is unimaginable and if for this reason we can have no idea of it, so also is God unimaginable and even finite spirits. So is not God also an unintelligible absurdity on Berkeley's own principles? This is a difficulty; Berkeley was aware of it and he tried to meet it. So the reader is asked for the present not to question Berkeley's accceptance of God and finite spirits but to consider only whether he can give a satisfactory account of commonsense belief and of science in terms of these spirits, their activities and their ideas.

Berkeley consistently claims that one of the great merits of his position is that it is wholly compatible with common sense. In his private notebooks he frequently reminds himself that he must emphasise this in his published work, as is clear from the following quotations:

> All things in the Scripture which side with the vulgar against the learned, side with me also. I side in all things with the mob.

> I must be very particular in explaining what is meant by things existing . . . when not perceived as well as when perceived; and shew how the vulgar notion agrees with mine.

> Mem. To be eternally banishing Metaphysics, etc., and recalling men to common sense.

> Mem. That I take notice that I do not fall in with the sceptics . . . in that I make bodies to exist certainly, which they doubt of. (C 405, 408, 751, 79)

In this claim he never wavers. Thus in the first of the dialogues between Hylas and Philonous he even makes conformity to common sense the touchstone of acceptability. 'Well then,' says Philonous, 'are you content to admit that opinion for true, which upon examination shall appear most agreeable to Common Sense, and remote from Scepticism?' (L ii 172). To this Hylas agrees.

In claiming that he is in accord with common sense Berkeley clearly cannot mean that the common man has always been aware of and has always accepted a philosophical position identical with his own. He himself says that while we should 'speak with the vulgar' we should 'think with the learned', and he acknowledges that 'it is indeed an opinion strangely prevailing among men, that houses, mountains, rivers, and in a word all sensible objects, have an existence, natural or real, distinct from their being perceived by the understanding' (P 4). This view, as distinct from the philosophical doctrine of matter, is clearly attributed to the common man by Berkeley, and with good reason. Rather, it appears, he is making the following twofold claim: first, that Berkeley himself is committed to no positive claims about the world which are not already assented to by common sense, unlike the followers of the corpuscularian philosophy, who have introduced imperceptible matter; secondly, that given any belief of common sense expressed in the common non-technical language of everyday life, he can provide an alternative statement of that belief in terms of his basic hypothesis, equivalent to the commonsense statement in the sense that it would be impossible to imagine a state of the world which would make one of them true when the other was false. Berkeley, it seems clear, was not claiming that the common man was already aware of these equivalent formulations before Berkeley formulated them. As we shall see, he himself had at times considerable difficulty in deciding what reformulation was most acceptable and accurate. He was claiming to be able to provide what such more modern philosophers as Susan Stebbing and John Wisdom would have called a metaphysical or new-level analysis of the statements of common sense, and, as G. E. Moore constantly said, one may know the truth of a statement and understand it without being able to give its analysis.

Berkeley, then, claims that he can give an adequate analysis of commonsense beliefs in terms of an infinite spirit – God – finite spirits and mind-dependent ideas. He is well aware of the apparent difficulties in this position and lists them in paragraphs 34 onwards in the *Principles*:

First, then, it will be objected that by the foregoing principles all that is real and substantial in nature is banished out of the world, and instead thereof a chimerical scheme of *ideas* takes place.

Secondly, it will be objected that there is a great difference betwixt real fire, for instance, and the idea of fire, betwixt dreaming or imagining oneself burnt, and actually being so.

Thirdly, it will be objected that we see things actually without or at a distance from us, and which consequently do not exist in the mind.

Fourthly, it will be objected that from the foregoing principles it follows things are every moment annihilated and created anew.

We can learn to understand Berkeley's position no better than by considering why, in his view, it is immune to these objections.

How, then, if there are but spirits and their ideas, can there be a distinction between a real world and the world of dreams, of fantasy and of illusion? Surely the difference is that the world of dreams or fantasy or illusion is indeed only within our minds, and the real world independent of them? But Berkeley denies this. The difference is not between mind-dependent ideas on the one hand and something outside the mind on the other but between ideas having a certain nature, relation to each other and relation to ourselves, and ideas having a quite different nature, relation to each other and relation to ourselves. First, they differ normally in their nature; the ideas of imagination or dreaming or memory are less strong, lively and distinct than those of sense which constitute the real world. Secondly, they differ in their relation to us; the ideas of imagination and memory are brought before our minds by our own decision, whereas the ideas of sense are independent of our will. I can decide to think about trees, for example, but whether I see a tree when I open my eyes is quite beyond my control. Thirdly, the ideas of sense have 'a steadiness, order and coherence, and are not excited at random, as those which are the effects of human wills often are, but in a regular train or series' (P 30). In dream, imagination or illusion anything can happen, but in the real world the train of ideas is determined by the laws of nature.

Berkeley cannot claim, nor does he need to claim, that all these three types of difference are always observable; unlike imagination, dream and illusion have a content over which we have no control, for example. But he does want to claim that at least one of these differences will always be present and that awareness of them is the way, the only way, in which reality can be distinguished from illusion or other forms of unreality. How, for example, does Macbeth determine that the dagger that he sees is unreal? Here are Shakespeare's words that he puts into the mouth of Macbeth:

> Is this a dagger which I see before me,
> The handle toward my hand? Come, let me clutch thee!
> I have thee not, and yet I see thee still.
> Art thou not, fatal vision, sensible
> To feeling as to sight? or art thou but
> A dagger of the mind, a false creation
> Proceeding from the heat-oppressed brain?

Clearly Macbeth determines that the dagger is an illusion, not by finding (how could he?) that it has a status independent of his mind, but by finding that his ideas of sight and touch lack the coherence which would be necessary for the experience to count as experience of reality. Berkeley wants to claim that he can make the distinctions that common sense makes in his own terms and that in fact common sense makes the distinctions in precisely the ways that he describes. So the distinction between reality and the merely subjective is not just *detected* by the features Berkeley has mentioned, acting as clues; certain trains of ideas *count as* experience of reality while others do not, 'by which is meant', Berkeley claims, 'that they are more affecting, orderly and distinct, and they are not fictions of the mind perceiving them' (P 36). To be real and to have these features are, for Berkeley, one and the same thing. Berkeley is giving a reductionist analysis, not giving us hints on how to check up on our experience.

This is an appropriate place to pause and make for the first, but not the last, time the point that there is an important distinction to be made between Berkeley's analysis of common-sense beliefs in terms of ideas and his metaphysics. Berkeley certainly thinks that the metaphysical explanation of why some ideas have coherence, liveliness and independence of our wills is because God, the infinite spirit, causes them. Thus metaphysically reality is to be explained in terms of the activity of God; but the analysis of what we mean when we ascribe reality to something does not contain, as we have seen, any reference to God. This distinction is often ignored and Berkeley is frequently represented as bringing God into his analysis when he does not. Berkeley gives on the whole what may be counted as a positivistic analysis of commonsense beliefs, a fact which is perfectly compatible with the fact that he offers a theocentric metaphysic to explain why our experience has the character that it has. We should not underestimate the importance of God in Berkeley's thought, but we also should not misrepresent Berkeley as holding that talk about chairs and tables is to be analysed as talk about the deity.

Berkeley's treatment of the third objection, that what we see is at a distance from us and therefore cannot be within our minds, is the occasion for us to consider very briefly Berkeley's *A New Theory of Vision*, in which he is concerned to state how by the sense of sight we are able to judge distance. Berkeley was clear that distance had to be judged and could not be seen: 'For, distance being a line directed endwise to the eye, it projects only one point in the fund of the eye, which point remains invariably the same, whether the distance be longer or shorter' (V 2). If we judge distance it is not, he holds, as some have thought, in virtue of the difference of the angles of the eye in binocular vision, for we are not aware of the angles of the eyes when we judge distance, nor do we need to be. Nor do we ultimately judge from sensations in the eye, such as, perhaps, a sense of strain when we look at a thing close up. For we rather learn from experience that we experience the strain when the object is close and so must have another means of determining that the object is close.

Berkeley's own solution to this problem is in terms of a correlation between sight and touch. In the *New Theory of Vision* he gives this solution as though by touch we were aware of objects outside us in a real physical space, since, as he says in the *Principles*, he is there concerned with vision alone and not with the fundamentals of epistemology. More accurately, we should speak of a correlation of ideas of touch with ideas of vision. Though we speak of being aware of shape by both sight and touch, Berkeley maintains that the visual idea of, say, a rectangle and a tactual idea of a rectangle are quite distinct and we learn only from experience that given the one idea the other will accompany it. A great controversy raged about a question which the Dublin lawyer Molyneux set in a letter to his friend Locke:

> Suppose a man born blind and now adult, and taught by his touch to distinguish between a cube and a sphere of the same metal, and nighly of the same bigness, so as to tell, when he felt one and the other, which is the cube, which the sphere. Suppose then the cube and sphere placed on a table, and the blind man to be made to see; query, whether by his sight, before he touched them, he could now distinguish and tell which is the globe, which the cube?

To this question Berkeley, like Locke and Molyneux himself, gave the unequivocal answer 'No.' Now if we suppose that it will take more time, in similar conditions, to get the tactual idea of something round than to get the tactual idea of something rectangular, then the visual idea of the rectangular will be regarded as more distant than the visual idea of the round. This correlation of sight and touch is fundamental, in Berkeley's view. But on this basis we learn to judge distance in terms of the visual appearances of things; thus if one thing having the general look of a ping-pong ball looks larger than something that looks like a tennis ball we shall judge the ping-pong ball to be much nearer.

Thus Berkeley claims that the judgement of distance does not require us to posit an external space. Furthermore the appearance of relative distance from us can be exhibited by objects of imagination, which no one supposes to be in some real space, just as much as by the objects of the senses.

What then of the fourth difficulty that Berkeley mentioned, about the continued existence of ordinary physical bodies like chairs and tables and mountains and rivers? This difficulty has been expressed in a well-known limerick:

> There was a young man who said 'God
> Must think it exceedingly odd
> If he finds that this tree
> Continues to be
> When there's no one about in the Quad.'

The author of this limerick, Monsignor Ronald Knox, also produced another limerick which purports to offer Berkeley's solution to the problem and runs as follows:

> Dear Sir:
>   Your astonishment's odd;
> I am always about in the Quad.
> And that's why the tree
> Will continue to be,
> Since observed by
>   *Yours faithfully*,
>   GOD.

This view, which makes Berkeley locate the continuous existence of bodies in their eternal and continuous perception by God, is, I suppose, the orthodox interpretation of Berkeley on this topic. But it is at best a misleading and inadequate account of Berkeley's view. Certainly Berkeley held that metaphysically the existence of unobserved trees depended on the activity of God; but then he held that metaphysically the existence of observed trees and finite observers depended on the activity of God. But, as has already been said, we must distinguish between Berkeley's metaphysical view that all existence was dependent on God and his analytical views about the meaning of statements. There is very little, if any, evidence that Berkeley believed that, when we assert the existence of some unobserved object, what we mean is something about the observations of God; there is, on the contrary, a lot of evidence that he did not. So the rest of this chapter will be devoted to the discovery of what his views on this topic were. How could Berkeley, the immaterialist, allow the commonsense assumption that bodies exist continuously, whether perceived or unperceived?

This inquiry is both instructive and amusing. For Berkeley's great insight had been the negative one of the non-existence of matter. His initial claim that this insight was compatible with common sense was an act of faith, for he had at that stage no idea what account he should give of bodies. He tried out many theories, some plausible and ingenious, some very crude and unconvincing, before giving his final answer to the question in the third and last of the dialogues between Hylas and Philonous.

We find a number of mutually incompatible and unplausible suggestions about the nature of body in the private notebooks. Here, for example is a particularly ill-conceived one:

> We see the house itself, the church itself; it being an idea and nothing more. The house itself, the church itself, is an idea, i.e. an object – immediate object – of thought. (C 427, 427a)

But, clearly, to identify an object with some single idea will not do. For if I look three times at what common sense would call a house I have, in Berkeley's terminology, three separate ideas; if we identify the house with the ideas then I shall have seen not one but three houses, each of which will have only a fleeting existence.

Here is another suggestion from the same notebooks, one almost as unfortunate as the one just considered:

> You ask me whether the books are in the study now, when no one is there to see them? I answer, Yes. You ask me, Are we not in the wrong for imagining things to exist when they are not actually perceived by the senses? I answer, No. The existence of our ideas consists in being perceiv'd, imagin'd, thought on. Whenever they are mentioned or discours'd of they are imagin'd & thought on. Therefore you can at no time ask me whether they exist or no, but by reason of that very question they must necessarily exist. (C 472)

The ghost of this argument continued to haunt Berkeley in later writing; but he had no sooner written it down than he began to feel uneasy about it. The next note reads as follows:

> But, say you, a chimaera does exist? I answer, it doth in one sense, i.e. it is imagin'd. But it must be well noted that existence is vulgarly restrain'd to actual perception, and that I use the word existence in a larger sense than ordinary. (C 473)

This is, at best, a very half-hearted defence from one who claims to side with the vulgar against the learned.

But, on the whole, these early notebooks incline to phenomenalism. Bodies are to be what they were for Mill in his classical formulation of phenomenalism, permanent possibilities of sensation. Just how honestly one could claim that phenomenalism coincided with common sense did worry Berkeley, as it has worried many other phenomenalists, but he tried to stifle these doubts, as the following quotation shows:

> Mem. To allow existence to colours in the dark . . . but not an actual existence. 'Tis prudent to correct men's mistakes without altering their language. This makes truth glide into their souls insensibly. Colours in the dark do exist really, i.e. were there light, or as soon as light comes, we shall see them, provided we open our eyes; and that whether we will or no. (C 185, 185a)

What he says about colours he also says about bodies:

> Bodies &c. do exist whether we think of 'em or no, they being taken in a twofold sense –
>   1. Collections of thoughts.
>   2. Collections of powers to cause these thoughts. (C 282)

If an explanation of what he means here by powers is needed, he immediately gives it, again in a purely positivistic vein:

> Bodies taken for powers do exist when not perceived; but this existence is not actual. When I say a power exists, no more is meant than that if in the light I open my eyes, and look that way, I shall see it, i.e. the body &c. (C 293a)

Even when Berkeley was writing the *Principles* he had still not really made up his mind what to say about the continued existence of bodies. Here we have a thoroughly phenomenalistic story:

> The table I write on I say exists; that is, I see and feel it; and if I were out of my study I should say it existed; meaning thereby that if I were in my study I might perceive it, or that some other spirit actually does perceive it. (P 3)

Here 'some other spirit' is written without the capitals which

Berkeley always uses when referring to God – it surely means merely 'somebody else' and not God specifically. But over the page in the sixth paragraph we get the one case that I have noticed of Berkeley putting forward the view assigned to him by Ronald Knox in the limerick quoted above. Having reaffirmed that nothing exists outside a mind, he says of bodies:

> Consequently so long as they are not actually perceived by me, or do not exist in my mind, or of any other created spirit, they must either have no existence at all, or else subsist in the mind of some Eternal Spirit. (P 60)

Here we do have the capital E and capital S. It is unambiguously stated that, when not perceived by finite spirits, bodies, if they exist at all, must be in the mind of God; and this obviously and flatly contradicts the phenomenalistic story he has already given, unless we can claim that Berkeley has without warning moved from analysis to metaphysics.

There are two principal objections to the analysis of statements about physical objects in terms of the ideas in the mind of God, independently of doubts about God's existence. First, it is surely clear that the statement that God does not exist but that there are unobserved physical objects is not self-contradictory, even if it is false; when we speak of physical objects we do not thereby say anything about God. The second objection arises from the Christian theology which Berkeley accepted and needs explaining at a little more length.

It is a commonplace of theology that God is eternal and unchanging. The notion of an unchanging person may be difficult, but for the present all we need to understand by it is that God does not in time come to have ideas or thoughts which he had not had previously. It is another commonplace of theology, based theologically on the first chapter of the book of Genesis but no doubt confirmable by paleontological investigation, that God created the inanimate – the earth, the sea and the heavenly bodies – before he created on earth any living creatures. But if the existence of physical bodies consists in their being objects in the mind of God, then physical objects have existed from all eternity and were not created at all; and the existence of physical objects can also not consist in their being actually ideas of finite spirits, since they were created before finite spirits.

So it would seem that if we accept the doctrine of creation, as Berkeley certainly did, the permanent existence of physical bodies cannot consist in their being actual objects of thought or perception either by an infinite or by finite spirits. It seems that Berkeley did not become fully aware of this problem until he wrote the three dialogues between Hylas and Philonous; there he meets it squarely in the third dialogue, and in doing so comes up with what, given his basic positions, philosophical and theological, must be the most satisfactory answer possible. The solution, stated baldly, is this; God has, indeed, all his ideas from all eternity, and this in no way constitutes the existence of physical bodies. When God created the physical universe his creation consisted in his ordaining that from that time forward ideas of the physical should be available to finite spirits if any; this ordinance was valid even before there were finite spirits, just as criminal laws are valid even if there are no criminals. So the existence of physical objects consists in the relevant ideas being available. Physical objects are permanent possibilities of sensation – that is the analysis – and this possibility exists because God ordains that it should – that is the metaphysical explanation of this possibility.

Thus the phenomenalist analysis prevails in the end, and in a form superior to earlier versions. Berkeley's phenomenalist analysis at the beginning of the *Principles*, already quoted, starts: 'The table I write on I say exists; that is, I see and feel it' (P 3). He goes on to allow for its existence when he is not in his study; but it surely is clear that we never (*never*) assert that we are actually observing an object when we assert its existence, even if as a matter of fact we are observing it. So as an analysis the account in terms of the possibility of ideas alone is clearly preferable and seems to be about the best version of phenomenalism that it is possible to formulate. On the whole it is true that the *Three Dialogues* are largely a more popular version of ideas that are more accurately and fully developed in the *Principles*. But when Berkeley, in the third dialogue, wrote: 'things, with regard to us, may properly be said to begin their existence, or be created, when God decreed they should become perceptible to intelligent creatures, in that order and manner which He then established, and we now call the laws of nature' (L ii 253), he was surely making an advance on what he had previously written.

We may close this chapter on Berkeley's view of the physical world with a look at a famous, or perhaps notorious, attempt by Berkeley to prove that it is impossible to conceive of bodies existing independently of minds. He repeats it more than once in very similar language and I quote it now from paragraph 23 of the *Principles*:

> But, say you, surely there is nothing easier than for me to imagine trees, for instance, in a park, or books existing in a closet, and nobody by to perceive them. I answer, you may so, there is no difficulty in it. But what is all this, I beseech you, more than framing in your mind certain ideas which you call *books* and *trees*, and at the same time omitting to frame the idea of any one that may perceive them? But do you not yourself perceive or think of them all the while? This therefore is nothing to the purpose; it only shews you have the power of imagining, or forming ideas in your mind; but it does not shew that you can conceive it possible the objects of your thought may exist without the mind. To make this out, it is necessary that you conceive them existing unconceived or unthought of; which is a manifest repugnancy.

This is surely fallacious; certainly it is not possible that a body be conceived of and at the same time both exist and not be conceived of, just as God cannot be conceived of and at the same time exist and not be conceived of, and just as a chair cannot be kicked and at the same time exist unkicked. If one is thinking of a chair then it does not exist unthought of. But this has no tendency to show that the concept of an unthought-of chair has any logical deficiencies.

So Berkeley cannot prove that it is logically necessary to concede that body is ultimately mind-dependent. But he can surely claim to have made a very plausible effort to show that his view gives common sense everything it needs. Our experience of the world, as it actually occurs, cannot be different from how it would be on a Berkeleian view, since our experience of it just is the sequence of ideas of which Berkeley speaks. Any apparent discrepancy will not disprove Berkeley's view in principle, but will merely show that it has been mis-stated. We might perhaps believe that we could catch Berkeley out by taking a photograph of the interior of a room by remote control when there is nobody in the room. But Berkeley is perfectly able to accept that we shall have the requisite series of ideas called looking at a photograph of an empty room in the given circumstances; that is part of the order of nature. Berkeley can well ask what more we want. Occam's razor tells us not to multiply entities beyond necessity, and all that Berkeley is taking away from us, he claims, is a hidden machinery which is a totally superfluous hypothesis, in so far as it is at all intelligible.

If we do imagine that Berkeley speaks to us in some such words as those we may be tempted to reply as follows: even if it be true that the hypothesis is superfluous at the level of everyday life, in science it is not superfluous. So far from the material world being a something we know not what, science is continually discovering more and more about it and, in virtue of our knowledge of its nature, we are able to predict and engineer new marvels which would otherwise be unknown. How could man make the atom bomb if there were no atoms, and how could he predict it from a superfluous and empty hypothesis? We might be tempted to say this because it is a very natural, not to say obvious, thing to say at this stage. Being natural and obvious, the thought has occurred to Berkeley also. Our objection would not have caught him unprepared and he answered it in advance to his own satisfaction. In the next chapter we shall examine what account of the nature of the empirical sciences Berkeley was able to give on his principles.

4 The nature of empirical science

'Mem. Much to recommend and approve of experimental philosophy' said Berkeley in his private notebooks (C 498). This was no piece of window-dressing. Berkeley's interest in experimental science, or experimental philosophy as he called it in accordance with normal seventeenth- and eighteenth-century usage, was intense and genuine. His great admiration for Newton is expressed over and over again in his writings, and not only in those intended for publication. He had studied Newton's *Principia* – a very difficult work which very few could claim to understand with any ease – and probably the *Optics*. He never doubted that most of the experimental discoveries of Newton were true and valuable additions to human knowledge. So on the whole Berkeley had no desire to argue with the experimental scientists; most of his endeavours were directed to showing that the findings of science could and should be interpreted in a way which made them perfectly in accord with his philosophy and did not demand a belief in the independent material world. Criticism of Newton's experimental work is almost entirely confined to that small portion in which Newton claims to find empirical grounds for asserting the existence of absolute space and motion. Berkeley also criticised the mathematics that Newton had developed to state his arguments, in particular the theory of fluxions, but this topic will be discussed in a later chapter. The most important parts of Berkeley's works to consult on experimental philosophy are *Principles* 101 – 17 and the essay *De motu (On Motion)*, which was originally published in Latin, but of which translations are available. There are also, as we shall see, some important remarks on the topic in Berkeley's very late work intriguingly entitled *Siris: a Chain of Philosophical Reflexions and Inquiries concerning the Virtues of Tar-Water*.

The complete title of the work we call the *Principles* ends with the phrase: 'wherein the chief causes of error and difficulty in the sciences, with the grounds of scepticism, athe-

ism, and irreligion, are inquired into'. The scepticism Berkeley
has in mind is not so much religious doubt, which he here calls
irreligion, but doubt about the possibility of knowledge about
the world, or scientific scepticism. The most obvious place for
doubt is concerning the reality of the physical world. Berkeley
claims that on his view the physical world is immediately available to the senses, so that there is no cause to doubt its existence; but if the world is to be an imperceptible and unimaginable matter distinct from the ideas we have, then there is cause
for doubt of its existence. As we have seen already, Locke's
official doctrine that 'since the mind . . . hath no immediate objects but its own ideas . . . it is evident that our knowledge is
only conversant about them' is plainly incompatible with knowledge of a reality beyond our ideas; when in Book IV, Chapter
iv of his *Essay*, entitled 'Of the Reality of Human Knowledge',
he tries to meet the objection that on his principles 'knowledge
placed in ideas may be all bare vision', the argument is notoriously weak, being little more than the claim that our simple
ideas must have some cause.

Furthermore, if we pass over the doubts concerning the
reality of matter, Locke himself insists that knowledge in the
physical sciences is virtually impossible. On Locke's view, the
true nature, or real essence, of physical things, depended on the
organisation of the basic atoms that composed them; but since
we do not have microscopic eyes, as he himself puts it, we can
never know this organisation and therefore never know why
bodies are as they are. And, he continues, even if we could
observe these insensible parts,

> we are so far from knowing what figure, size, or motion of
> parts produce a yellow colour, a sweet taste, or a sharp
> sound, that we can by no means conceive how any size,
> figure, or motion of any particles can possibly produce in us
> the idea of any colour, taste, or sound whatever; there is no
> conceivable connexion betwixt the one and the other. In vain
> therefore shall we endeavour to discover by our ideas (the
> only true way of certain and universal knowledge) what other
> ideas are to be found constantly joined with that of our com-
> plex idea of any substance.

So Berkeley's first point in defence of his conception of science is in effect a preventive or spoiling attack. If the physical world is a transcendent reality inaccessible to our investigation scientific knowledge is impossible. Since on Berkeley's view the physical world was directly accessible, the possibility of knowledge about it did not meet such basic problems.

Locke' theory not only made physical reality inaccessible; it also ascribed causal agency to this inaccessible organisation of particles. Berkeley denied all causal efficacy to anything in the physical world, which was, on his analysis, ultimately composed of ideas alone. Paragraphs 25 and 26 of the *Principles* contain the clearest statement of his grounds for this view, which is revealed in the following quotations from those paragraphs:

> All our ideas . . . are visibly inactive . . . so that one idea . . . cannot produce or make any alteration in another . . . For, since they and every part of them exist only in the mind, it follows that there is nothing in them but what is perceived; but whoever shall attend to his ideas, whether of sense or reflexion, will not perceive in them any power or activity . . . Whence it plainly follows that extension, figure and motion cannot be the cause of our sensations . . . We perceive a continual succession of ideas.

Since these ideas do not cause each other they must be caused by the only kind of agency we know, a spirit.

It is worthwhile to compare this claim with the views of Hume. Hume agrees with Berkeley that we can find in nature nothing beyond succession; there is in nature no causal relation beyond succession. But whereas Berkeley goes on to claim that we must therefore locate true causal agency elsewhere, in spirits, Hume takes a different line; since we can find no causal agency in nature beyond succession we must analyse causation in terms of succession; causation is nothing more than the regular succession which we observe in nature; the constant conjunction of ideas which we experience produces an inevitable expectation in our minds of the continuance of the regularity and we transfer this inevitability into the realm of nature by a kind of illusion. Here Hume is carrying the line of reductionist analysis started by Berkeley further than Berkeley (whom Hume greatly admired) was prepared to go. Part of the explanation is that Hume denied Berkeley's claim, vital to his metaphysics, that he could distinguish a genuine activity in spirits going beyond mere succession; we shall have to consider this problem carefully when we come to look closely at Berkeley's account of spirits and their powers.

Science, then, for Berkeley, is not investigating a nature beyond our ideas or discovering causal connections, either between matter and matter, or matter and ideas, or ideas and ideas. What then is the role of the scientist or experimental philosopher? Berkeley's basic answer is given in paragraph 105 of the *Principles*:

> If therefore we consider the difference there is betwixt natural philosophers and other men, with regard to their knowledge of the phenomena, we shall find it consists, not in an exacter knowledge of the efficient cause that produces them – for that can be no other than the *will of a spirit* – but only in a greater largeness of comprehension, whereby analogies, harmonies, and agreements are discovered in the works of nature, and the particular effects explained, that is, reduced to general rules.

At this point we must insist once again on the distinction between Berkeley's analytic theories and his metaphysics. Metaphysically the explanation of why the world is as it is, the causal agency which maintains it as it is, the ground which permits us to ask for final causes (What is it for?) in nature, must be a spirit, whom Berkeley calls God. Metaphysically, therefore, scientists are investigating the handiwork of God, reading the divine handwriting, as Berkeley sometimes puts it, discovering the designs of God. But, given this metaphysical basis, we must give a different analytical account of what the scientist is doing. Metaphysically all scientists are investigating the activity of God, but analysis must allow that one is investigating an alkali and another an acid; metaphysically the explanation of every phenomenon is God, but we must give an analytic account of science which allows that the explanation of one natural phenomenon will often be very different from the explanation of another.

If we now ask for an account of Berkeley's basic analysis of the nature of empirical science, the answer is that the scientist is discovering regularities in the succession of our ideas. In so doing he is doing nothing different in principle from what all men do when they learn from experience. He is merely doing it in a much more systematic way. But Berkeley also gives an analytic account of scientific explanation which, simply stated, is the reduction to general rules. We may usefully clarify and explain this doctrine with the use of one of Berkeley's own examples.

That apples, and not only apples, fall to the ground, that tides are affected by the moon, that the moon circles the earth and that the planets rotate round the sun – these and similar phenomena were all well known and familiar to men before Newton. What Newton did was not to discover these phenomena but to explain them. He explained them by showing them all to be special cases of a single regularity – gravitational attraction. Unlike Newton, but like many of Newton's earliest and closest disciples, we may be tempted to regard this as explanation by reference to some efficient cause, some force called the force of gravitation. But as an efficient cause the force of gravitation would be a mere something we knew not what; to say that apples accelerate towards the earth at a rate of thirty-two feet per second per second because there is a force that accelerates them at that rate is empty talk, as it would be to say that petrol in an internal combustion engine ignites because it has a power of combustion. What Newton did to explain these and related phenomena was to show that they were all cases of the same few basic principles. Gravitational attraction is a concept which has explanatory power because it is a shorthand way of referring to the common feature exhibited by all these phenomena, not because it names an efficient cause of them. So explanation is neither the giving of an efficient cause or mere description but, in Berkeley's words, 'reduction to general rules'.

If we turn to *De motu*, we shall find a further amplification of this analysis of science, an analysis which in recent years has attracted more attention than earlier, since philosophers have noticed in it similarities to the positivist analysis of the nature of mechanical science by the nineteenth-century Austrian philosopher and physicist, Mach. In *De motu* Berkeley is mainly concerned with the science of mechanics, the only part of science which in his day had achieved a mathematical formulation and systemisation. In mechanics one uses constantly such terms as 'mass', 'force', 'momentum' and 'energy'; are we to say that this is illegitimate, and how can we avoid doing so, if we start from Berkeley's immaterialist basis? Since *De motu* is not so easily accessible as the *Principles* and the *Dialogues*, let us read Berkeley's solution so far as possible in a translation of his own words:

> *Force*, *gravity*, *attraction*, and words of this sort are useful for reasoning and computations concerning motion and bodies in motion; but not for understanding the simple nature of motion itself or for designating so many distinct qualities. (M 17)

> For understanding the true nature of motion it will be of the greatest assistance first, to distinguish between mathematical models and the nature of things: secondly, to beware of abstractions: thirdly, to consider motion as something sensible, or at least imaginable; and to be content with relative measurements. If we do these things, not only will all the celebrated theorems of mechanics, by which the secrets of nature are revealed and the system of the world is subjected to human calculation, remain unimpaired, but also the study of motion will escape free from a thousand pedantries, subtleties and abstract ideas. (M 66)

> All forces attributed to bodies are as much mathematical hypotheses as attractive forces in the planets and the sun. Moreover mathematical entities have no firm essence in the world of nature, but they depend on the notions of him who defines them, so that the same thing can be explained in various ways. (M 67)

> The mechanical principles and universal laws of motion so happily discovered in the last century, stated and applied with the aid of geometry, introduced a remarkable clarity into science. But the metaphysical principles and the true efficient

causes of motion and of the existence of bodies or the properties of bodies are in no way part of mechanics or experimental science. (M 41)

Thus we find Berkeley giving a completely positivistic analysis of science, while maintaining a theistic explanation at the
metaphysical level. In so far as science is talking about observed
phenomena (sensible ideas) or, at least, objects of possible experience (the imaginable), we may take it literally. Berkeley
does not wish to doubt the existence of small particles, regarded
in the way he regards all bodies, as permanent possibilities of
sensation. But in so far as science wishes to talk of inherently
imperceptible bodies, this is legitimate for computational purposes but must not be taken literally.

What Berkeley has in mind when he speaks of mathematical
models or hypotheses as having no real existence and as depend-
ing for their content on the arbitrary definition of the scientist
can be explained by reference to an illustration he himself uses
in *Siris*. Ptolemy in his geocentric astronomy accounted for the
motion of the heavenly bodies by means of a theory of cycles
and epicycles (circles revolving round a circle). This he did so
successfully that users of the heliocentric astronomy did not
succeed in accounting significantly better for the motions of the
stars and calculating their courses until about the time of Newton. Now the hypothesis of epicycles can be indefinitely refined
to account with increasing accuracy for celestial motions. Is,
then, the heliocentric or the geocentric hypothesis correct? Are
there or are there not epicycles? Berkeley's answer to this question would be that both theories are mathematical hypotheses
and, in so far as they answer equally well empirical questions
about what we shall observe, it is senseless to ask which is true.
It is legitimate to talk about epicycles, or gravity, provided that
we realise that to do so is merely to adopt one framework for
computation rather than another. Here are Berkeley' own words
on this topic:

It is one thing to arrive at general laws of nature from a con-
templation of the phenomena; and another to frame an
hypothesis, and from thence deduce the phenomena. Those
who suppose epicycles, and by them explain the motions and

appearances of the planets, may not therefore be thought to have discovered principles true in fact and nature. And, albeit we may from the premises infer a conclusion, it will not follow that we can argue reciprocally, and from the conclusion infer the premises. (S 228)

There is much of interest in *Siris* for the student of Berkeley's philosophy of science, particularly in sections 247 and following.

Berkeley, then, thought that he could give an adequate analysis of science in terms of his basic phenomenalistic view. This analysis has to be supplemented according to Berkeley by a metaphysic. Since there is no causal agency within nature we must account for the regularity and very existence of the world of nature by an agency lying outside it, which is, according to Berkeley, an incomparably powerful spirit that he calls God. Berkeley's view of spirits and of the Infinite Spirit on which his metaphysical explanation of the possibility of science depends will be considered in detail later. But one consequence of this metaphysic may be considered now, Berkeley's defence of seeking final causes within science.

Plato and Aristotle, and their medieval followers, had insisted on the importance of final causes in science. An important part, they would have said, of understanding, say, the heart or the liver is understanding what purpose it serves. Just how far teleological explanation is to be sought was not clear; Aristotle himself explicitly said that there was no teleological explanation of such facts as that rain fell at some particular place and time. But certainly some teleological explanation was part of science. That teleological explanation was possible was not doubted by the Christian philosophers and scientists of the late seventeenth century; but the pious Boyle himself laid it down that there should be no reference to God in the explanation of particular phenomena. God had created matter which behaved according to immutable laws, and it was illegitimate to explain the behaviour of anything in science except by reference to matter and the universal laws of its behaviour. But Berkeley was dissatisfied with this. It would be an extreme behaviourist who rejected teleological explanation of intelligent human activity; to ask to what end you or I acted in a certain way seems obviously justified and an answer is surely needed if we are to understand that action. But if we regard the natural world as the direct and immediate activity of God surely the same teleological question will be appropriate here, even if we cannot always find the answer. Why should the fact that God acts in a reliably predictable manner prohibit the question? It is not that Berkeley wants questions about God to be regarded as part of natural science; we know that he did not. But he thought that the metaphysical propriety of speaking of God's purposes meant that it was appropriate to ask within science to what end the liver or heart behaved as it did and to regard it as possible to answer such questions. The modern scientist seems to preach the doctrine of Boyle rather than that of Berkeley on this topic, though whether in fact we shall ever cease to ask and answer such teleological questions about natural phenomena, or some of them, is another matter.

So far Berkeley has been giving his interpretation of the activities of Newton, not condemning them. He has censured Newton's followers for thinking of attraction as a real entity to explain motion, but he has explicitly excepted Newton from this error. But to some of Newton's doctrines Berkeley did take exception, and on topics about which modern scientists are more likely to agree with Berkeley than with Newton. In particular Newton had distinguished absolute time and space from relative time and space in a celebrated scholium in the *Principia*:

> Absolute, true, and mathematical time, of itself and from its own nature, flows equably without relation to anything external . . .

> Absolute space in its own nature, without relation to anything external, remains always similar and immovable . . .

How it can even make sense to speak of time flowing with a speed, constant or inconstant, Newton does not tell us. But he not only claims to be able to make the distinction conceptually between, say, our movement relative to the earth and the movement of the earth through absolute space; he even produces the celebrated bucket experiment as an empirical proof of the difference between the two. He claims that the varying behaviour of water in a bucket which is suddenly set into circular motion, the surface gradually becoming concave, has to be analysed by a distinction between the movement of the water relative to the bucket and its absolute motion.

Among scientists Newton's authority was so great that these distinctions were not challenged by them until the late nineteenth century, when Clerk Maxwell, Mach and then Einstein demolished them, presumably for ever. Leibniz had attacked them in a celebrated correspondence with Clarke, a close follower of Newton, but without much effect. Berkeley, too, saw that he had to attack Newton on this point, for a real absolute space, which Newton was even heretically willing to call the sensorium, or organ of perception, of God, could by no means be incorporated into a phenomenalistic account of science. Berkeley's attack is to be found in *Principles* 110–18; and it is what one would expect. He claims that the concepts of absolute space and time are empty and that what Newton regards as cases where the distinction between the absolute and the relative is required are shown to be cases where we have space or time relative to two different frames of reference. He in effect offers the modern solution to Newton's bucket experiment, that what Newton calls absolute motion is in fact motion relative to the fixed stars, so called. It is hard not to accept Berkeley as clearly right on this point, and hard to understand why his arguments were so long ignored.

Berkeley's philosophy of science was in his day totally novel. Few if any concurred with him until the rise of positivism in the late nineteenth century, but many philosophers and not a few scientists have accepted positions not unlike his in the twentieth century. As modern physics began to ascribe to its basic particles a character more and more unlike that of any objects with which we are acquainted with in experience, it became more and more satisfying to say that so long as the mathematical calculations led to correct predictions we should not ask for more and should regard the bewildering descriptions of fundamental particles as the inevitable result of trying to express non-mathematically what could only be expressed in mathematical terms. We should not regard a mathematical model as a factual description. Perhaps this is an over-simple view which sees too sharp a distinction between model or mathematical hypothesis and mere factual description; but certainly we cannot regard Berkeley's views as the eccentric dream of a crazy metaphysician.

5 God and finite spirits

There is surprisingly little said about spirits and their nature in either the *Principles* or the *Dialogues*. Why this is so is unclear. In the private notebooks Berkeley wrote: 'Mem. Carefully to omit defining of person, or making much mention of it' (C 713). Since he wrote just below: 'N.B. To use utmost caution not to give the least handle of offence to the Church or Churchmen' (C 715), it might be conjectured that it was out of prudence that he pursued this policy. But, again, when the first edition of the *Principles* appeared it was called 'Part I', though no Part II ever appeared. In a letter to an American friend named Samuel Johnson, Berkeley said that he had 'made considerable progress on the Second Part', adding that the manuscript 'was lost about fourteen years ago, during my travels in Italy; and I never had leisure since to do so disagreeable a thing as writing twice on the same subject'. Some have conjectured that we should have learnt more about spirits from this second part, though Berkeley alleges that *Principles* I, 135 to the end, deal with this topic.

The little that is said has often been thought to be unsatisfactory, so that the, surely unworthy, suspicion has been entertained that Berkeley says so little about spirits because he sees that his views on the topic are indefensible and inconsistent with what he says on other topics. It would be as well to start by indicating what the grounds for this dissatisfaction are.

It will be remembered that Berkeley opened the *Principles* with the assertion that it is evident that the objects of human knowledge are limited to ideas of sense, ideas of passions and other operations of the mind, and ideas of memory and imagination. But while we may observe our passions, our thoughts and our planning, and other 'operations of the mind', we never observe, that is, have an idea of, the mind itself. Some twenty-two or twenty-three years later Hume was to write: 'For my part, when I enter most intimately into what I call *myself*, I always stumble on some particular perception or other, of heat or cold, light or shade, love or hatred, pain or pleasure.' So Hume, on the same phenomenalist principle that Berkeley follows in analysing physical bodies, reduces the person to a series of ideas and sensations. How can Berkeley do otherwise? And, if he does so, is he to give a similar phenomenalist account of the infinite spirit who may be called God?

Berkeley is perfectly well aware of this problem. But he has no thought of trying to avoid it by claiming that he has an idea of himself. He agrees entirely with Hume that there is nothing that can be an object of attention which could be called the thinker of the thought or the feeler of the pain as one is aware of the thought or the pain. Berkeley states the problem in this way in the *Principles*: 'But it will be objected that, if there is no *idea* signified by the terms *soul*, *spirit*, and *substance*, they are wholly insignificant, or have no meaning in them' (P 139). Then in the next paragraph he says: 'In a large sense indeed, we may be said to have an idea or rather a notion of *spirit*. That is, we understand the meaning of the word, otherwise we could not affirm or deny anything of it.' This is very easily seen as a mere evasion of the problem. It is not clear why Locke and Newton should not reply to Berkeley that perhaps they have no idea of matter in a narrow sense but that in a larger sense they have an idea or rather notion of it in so far as they understand the word *matter* as readily as Berkeley understands the word *spirit*. Moreover it is not clear that God as an ultimate metaphysical explanation of things is essentially different from matter; in each case the metaphysical source of ideas is to be a something that causes ideas of which itself we can have no proper idea. An appeal to a transcendent something we know not what is perhaps equally futile by whatever name we call that something. Such is the difficulty; we must look carefully to see whether Berkeley's position is really as weak as it can certainly appear.

If we read the entries in Berkeley's private notebooks that are concerned with minds, souls or spirits, it is clear that he was initially in some doubt what line to take. This wavering can be graphically illustrated. At one point he writes: 'We think we know not the soul, because we have no imaginable or sensible idea annex'd to that sound. This the effect of prejudice' (C 576). But then in the very next entry he contradicts himself:

'Certainly we do not know it' (C 576a).

At this point Berkeley adopts a position he will later abandon, one which anticipates the Humean notion of the mind as a bundle or series of ideas. The passage deserves an extended quotation:

> The very existence of ideas constitutes the Soul. Consciousness, perception, existence of ideas, seem to be all one . . .
>
> Consult, ransack your understanding. What find you there besides several perceptions or thoughts? What mean you by the word mind? You must mean something that you perceive, or that you do not perceive. A thing not perceived is a contradiction. To mean (also) a thing you do not perceive is a contradiction. We are in all this matter strangely abused by words. Mind is a congeries of perceptions. Take away perceptions and you take away the mind. Put the perceptions and you put the mind. (C 577, 579–80)

At this stage he is so bold as to say that 'in sleep and in trances the mind *exists not*', since its existence is identical with the occurrence of ideas.

We have seen that Berkeley has shown himself well aware of the problem how spirits can be accounted for on his basic premises; and we have seen him willing to canvass a view of the mind which has often been regarded as one of Hume's most daring innovations. This being so, we can scarcely explain his apparently weak claim in the *Principles* that we have a notion of spirit, though no idea of it, as arising from either an inability to see its apparent weakness or from a mere timid evasion of the problem. In fact he does seem to have believed himself to have discovered a true theory of the nature of spirits which does overcome the basic difficulty, and this view we must now examine.

Perhaps the shortest way to put Berkeley's position, though it is not Berkeley's own, is to say that we know ideas as objects of observation; we cannot observe ourselves and so we are not ideas and we have no idea of ourselves; but we do act, and will and observe, and it is this activity which constitutes our existence as spirits. In Berkeley's language, the existence of ideas consists in their being perceived (their *esse* is *percipi*), whereas the existence of spirits consists in acting, willing and perceiving (their esse is *agere, velle, percipere*). 'By the word *spirit* we mean only that which thinks, wills and perceives' (P 138).

So we are aware of ourselves as acting, not by observation but simply because action is a conscious activity. Berkeley claims that we are actually aware of our causal agency, of our exertion of power. Hume will deny this, partly by claiming that we have no idea of power or force – which Berkeley himself urges – and partly by pointing out that even when we will to perform some simple action we may fail to do so (our arm may be paralysed when we try to move it). But the cases that Berkeley has in mind are not of bodily events but of our summoning up ideas in our minds. We are not aware of some phenomenon called the exertion of power, but we consciously exert power when we call any train of thought or imagination before our minds.

So we understand the word 'spirit', which Berkeley calls 'having a notion of spirit', though we have no idea of spirit in the strict sense of idea. Spirits are substances; they are that in the world which acts and ideas are the field of their actions, totally inert and mind-dependent.

This immediate awareness of ourselves as spirits is unique. We are not aware even of other spirits in this way. Berkeley says very little about our knowledge of other minds, a topic which has received much very sophisticated attention from recent philosophers. He is content with a simple argument from analogy – we attribute an active finite spirit which governs it to each body which behaves like ours. This has been much attacked as a form of argument – by F. H. Bradley on the ground that we do not want as friends inferred beings who are mere hypotheses to explain physical phenomena, and by others on the ground that the analogy is weak, being from one case to all, or illegitimate in principle. This is not the place to go into this question, to which Berkeley allowed only a few perfunctory words.

Berkeley uses this conception of finite spirits to argue for the natural immortality of the soul in a manner reminiscent of Plato's *Phaedo*. When bodies cease to exist what happens is that they are dissolved into their constituent parts or elements in accordance with the laws of nature. Since to perish is the dissolution of a complex into its simple parts, we can have no idea of the perishing of something simple. But the soul is 'indivisible, incorporal, unextended'; it is therefore, not being part of nature, not subject to the laws of nature, and, being simple, is not capable of dissolution. God can create a soul or annihilate it, but apart from the creative power of God nothing comes to be out of nothing or becomes nothing. Once again, Berkeley gives this argument without any attempt at elaboration or defence against possible objections and we shall not pursue the topic here.

But what of the existence of God? For the whole of Berkeley's metaphysics depends on his existence. Berkeley's argument is basically very simple: he, Berkeley, is aware of ideas in his own mind and knows them to be essentially dependent on the mind. The notion of a pain or a sound or a tickle or even a coloured expanse existing independently of a mind is absurd. But while Berkeley is conscious that the existence of some ideas is dependent on his mind and on his will, it is manifest that the great bulk of ideas are not dependent for their existence or character on his own mind; nor could they be caused by another mind similar in capacity to Berkeley's own; nor, being clearly passive and mind-dependent, could they be permanent, independent and basic entities. The mind that must therefore be causally responsible for the existence of that regular sequence of ideas that we call reality must be immensely more powerful than our own.

This argument is clearly a version of the cosmological argument, an argument from the existence of the world to a cause of its existence. But it has its own special features. Thus, one common reply to the cosmological argument has always been to ask why we need to ask for a cause of the existence of the world, which might be treated as basic just as easily as a creator could be treated as basic. But Berkeley can reply to this that on his view the natural world is known to be essentially mind-dependent; the only question can be on what mind it is so dependent. Why Berkeley is entitled, if he is, to call the mind that is responsible for the natural order an infinite spirit rather than merely a very powerful spirit, why he should be entitled to call this spirit eternal, and why he should be entitled to identify it with the God of the Christian religion, are further and difficult questions. But the notion of some very powerful mind that must be responsible for the world-order is deeply embedded in Berkeley's views and it cannot be excised as a mere religious excrescence arbitrarily added by a future bishop.

I have emphasised the importance of the infinite spirit in Berkeley's philosophy as the cause of those regular sequences of ideas that are called reality. Berkeley is often represented as arguing that God is needed to keep the world in existence by perceiving it. That Berkeley did believe that God in some sense perceives the world is clear; but I do not believe that Berkeley held the view, which Malebranche held, that what we perceive is the ideas of God. What makes the natural world and its order is the will of God that men should obtain these ideas, not God's own perception of them from all eternity.

Berkeley often referred to the natural course of ideas as the language or handwriting of God. He wanted this to be taken very literally, so much so that it is a central element in an argument for the existence of God produced in the dialogue *Alciphron*. In this dialogue a Christian, Euphranor, and Alciphron, a free-thinker, or minute philosopher, as Berkeley prefers to call him, are the main characters. In the fourth of these dialogues Euphranor presses Alciphron to explain why he believes in other finite spirits, though imperceptible, but does not believe in God. Alciphron replies that though he cannot perceive other finite spirits he has empirical evidence for their existence since he can communicate with them; Alciphron, in effect, produces the argument from analogy on which Berkeley himself had relied in the *Principles*. Euphranor now says: 'But if it should appear plainly that God speaks to men by the intervention and use of arbitrary, outward, sensible signs, having no resemblance or necessary connexion with the things they stand for and suggest . . . will this content you?' (A iv 7). He then proceeds to claim that the relation between cause and effect, or between visible appearance and feel, is as arbitrary as between any word and its signification; 'you have as much reason to think the Universal Agent or God speaks to your eyes, as you can have for thinking any particular person speaks to your ears' (A iv 12); the look of fire is God's warning to us of potential danger in exactly the same way as is a human shout of 'Fire!'. So Alciphron is made to acknowledge that 'we see God with our fleshly eyes as plain as we see any human person whatsoever, and that He daily speaks to our senses in a manifest and clear dialect'. Whether Alciphron ought to have found this argument so convincing is another question, but it is interesting in its literal use of the notion of sensible ideas being literally a sign-language to warn and inform us of other experience, as well as for its novel use of the argument from analogy for the existence of other minds.

We should, in our consideration of Berkeley on minds or spirits, finally note a problem for Berkeley which is one facet of the problem of free will and determinism which besets all philosophers, whether idealist or materialist, theistic or atheistic. It will be remembered that Berkeley distinguished the world of imagination from the real world by claiming that, metaphysically, God was the cause of the occurrence of the ideas which constitute the real world while finite spirits are the cause of their own ideas or imagination; the same distinction can be made by the empirical observation that we can choose to imagine or not to imagine, whereas the ideas that constitute reality are beyond our control; that the ideas of imagination are fragmentary and disordered, whereas the ideas that constitute reality are orderly and continuous; and the ideas of imagination are less lively and vivid than the ideas that constitute reality. So the whole distinction between reality and the world of fantasy depends on the view that ideas constituting reality are caused by God, and are outside our control.

What, then, is Berkeley to say about our own bodily movements? It would seem that the series of ideas which constitute the history of a human body are philosophically on a par with the series of ideas which constitute the history of any other real body. So must not the series of ideas that constitute the movement of a part of my body be caused by God and so be outside my control? But if this is so, are we committed to the view that man has no control over his bodily movements, that as causal agents we can control only the activities of our imaginations?

Berkeley was not willing to accept this view. In the private notebooks, the first writings of Berkeley that we have, he wrote:

'We move our legs ourselves. 'Tis we that will their movement' (C 548), and in his very last book, *Siris*, there is some strange neo-Platonic speculation about how the soul moves the body. There is no place where he departs from this view, but also no place where he deals with the problems that it raises, so that we can only speculate on what answer he would give on this point if pressed.

Part of the difficulty could perhaps be fairly easily dealt with. It is clear that in one way we always have some control over the course of our ideas; we can open or shut our eyes, turn our heads in one direction or another, and so on. It is clear that in saying that we cannot choose what ideas of reality we shall experience Berkeley means that if we open our eyes or turn our heads in a particular direction we shall see what we shall see and cannot choose how things will look; he does not need to deny that we can choose whether to look in order to make the distinction between reality and the world of imagination. Perhaps Berkeley could argue that we can will to move our leg just as we can will to look or turn our heads, and what we shall then see, the ideas that we shall have, is in each case equally outside our control. To put the point another way, there are many different possible series of ideas which might occur in our life-histories, each of which would be equally part of reality. We may, for example, choose to sit and watch one television programme or another, or to watch no television at all; but, though we can, so to speak, choose between different programmes, we cannot determine the content of the programme which we have chosen; whereas in imagination the programme is indefinitely variable at will. Perhaps Berkeley could maintain that his answer to the objection that 'by the foregoing principles all that is real and substantial in nature is banished out of the world' might be justified in this way.

But serious difficulties remain. Berkeley would allow that God from time to time brought about a miracle which was an exception to the regularity of nature; but he held that in general nature was uniform and that this uniformity was part of the goodness of God, through which one experience could be reliably expected on the basis of another. How could a human decision to move or not to move a leg be compatible with such uniformity? This is the Berkeleian version of the ancient problem how free will can be compatible with the uniformity of nature. There is also the problem how a finite will is to cause the Infinite Spirit to bring about one series of ideas rather than another, which is the Berkeleian version of the problem of how a will could act upon nature.

As we know, Berkeley deliberately abstained from discussing these problems in his published works, and we do not know whether he would have discussed them in the projected second part of the *Principles*. I suspect that Berkeley, like everyone else, would have had no adequate solution to offer and that this fact would not have shaken him. In the dialogues between Hylas and Philonous Hylas asks how Philonous can claim both that God was eternally unchanging and that God created the world; Philonous replies that he has no answer to this problem but does not need to answer it since it is a problem for all theists who accept the doctrine of creation and does not arise from the thesis of immaterialism. I suspect that on the problem of the freedom of the will Berkeley himself would have admitted that he had no clear answer to it but that it, too, was one which was common to all and in no way a special problem for him.

6 Mathematics

There are two distinct topics that must be considered in this chapter. First we shall consider Berkeley's own positive philosophy of mathematics, in which he attempts to give an account of the nature of mathematical propositions; secondly we must look at Berkeley's attacks on the mathematicians of his day, including the mighty Newton, for what Berkeley claimed were logical errors which invalidated both Newton's theory of fluxions and the equivalent infinitesimal calculus of Leibniz.

In his earlier writings, comprising remarks in his notebooks and paragraphs 118–32 of the *Principles*, Berkeley gave entirely different accounts of the nature of arithmetic and algebra on the one hand, and geometry on the other. The account of arithmetic and algebra he adhered to; the most implausible account of geometry he later abandoned in favour of an account which was very similar to that of arithmetic.

Berkeley held what would now be called a formalistic view of arithmetic and algebra. He held, as we have seen, that words stand for ideas – we can ask what they denote. But this is not so in the case of numerals; 'there are no *ideas* of number in the abstract, denoted by the numeral names'; arithmetical theorems have value because they can be applied, but 'can be supposed to having nothing at all for their object' (P 120). To say there are ten fish in a pool is nothing more than a compendious way of saying that there are as many fish in the pool as there are here strokes on the paper: / / / / / / / / / /. If there are ten fish in that pool, seven in another and twelve in a third, the principles of addition give us a convenient, quick method of determining the total number of fish. 'Hence', Berkeley says, 'we may see how entirely the science of numbers is subordinate to practice, and how jejune and trifling it becomes when considered as a matter of mere speculation' (P 120). This view will be distasteful to pure mathematicians; Berkeley's libel may be mitigated by the fact that in his youth he was an addict of pure mathematics. He even published a short Latin work on mathematics in 1707 containing a description of an algebraic game that he had invented.

By the time that he wrote *De motu* Berkeley had come to hold a view of geometry very similar to his view of arithmetic. We have seen, in discussing Berkeley's view of science, that though such terms as *attraction, action* and *force* are held to denote nothing real they are of the utmost value in computations of motion. In paragraph 39 of *De motu* he says that geometers also 'bring in many things for the development of their science that they cannot describe or find in the realm of nature which are of similar utility for computational purposes'.

But in earlier years Berkeley had held that geometry was an empirical science having as its subject-matter physical lines, triangles etc. Since physical things are, for Berkeley, merely bundles of ideas, geometry is in the end about our ideas of lines and the like. So construed, a point must be what he called a *minimum sensibile*, the smallest perceptible area, and all lines must have a finite length. A line so thought of is made up of points. Berkeley was prepared to accept the consequences. A line consisting of an odd number of points could not be bisected, he held; in his notebook he wrote: 'I say there are no incommensurables'; of the proof of congruence by superposition: 'the under triangle is no triangle – nothing at all, not being perceiv'd'; 'particular circles may be squared, for the circumference being given a diameter may be found betwixt which and the true there is no perceivable difference'; 'the diagonal is commensurable with the side' (C 469, 528, 249, 286).

Berkeley was well aware that these views had the sound of absurd paradox. But he thought that it was less absurd to hold his view than to hold that, for example, the word 'line' named something real which had length but no breadth; we have already seen that he regarded the claim that we have an abstract idea of length without breadth as merely to pile one absurdity on another. Abstract ideas are philosophical monstrosities. But his views were very odd, and as soon as he saw how to give an account of geometry which did not lead to these absurdities, as he saw them, he abandoned his own paradoxes.

In Berkeley's own time his positive views on the nature of

mathematics were given little heed. But in 1734 he published a polemical work on mathematics which in his lifetime was more celebrated than any other writing of his to that date, though *Siris* was later to outstrip it. This book was the occasion of a pamphlet war in which many of the leading mathematicians of the day took part. So though Berkeley's attack is of only historical interest and irrelevant to modern mathematics, we should pay some attention to it.

The full title of this book was *The Analyst; or a Discourse Addressed to an Infidel Mathematician wherein is examined whether the Object, Principles and Inferences of the Modern Analysis are more distinctly conceived, or more evidently deduced, than Religious Mysteries*. This title is significant; Berkeley's main aim is to show that free-thinking mathematicians, such as Edmund Halley, the famous astronomer, who mocked at the absurdities of Christian theology, were themselves guilty of logical errors of such seriousness that theology was of exemplary clarity in comparison with their mathematics. The subordinate aim, which was the means to the higher end, was to show that the mathematical analysis of his time was logically faulty; to achieve this he had to attack not only free-thinking mathematicians like Halley, but also such eminent theists as Newton, the inventor of the theory of fluxions, and Leibniz, who invented the equivalent theory of the infinitesimal calculus. The theory of fluxions, or of differential calculus, is a method of determining the rate of change of one variable in relation to another; since such concepts as that of acceleration are of rates of change, the theory was of vital importance to Newton's presentation of mechanics in mathematical form.

Berkeley objected in any case, as we have seen, to talk of infinitely short lines or extensionless points, but that is not the main point of attack in the *Analyst*; his objection here is that the mathematicians of his day were guilty of enormous logical howlers in their argumentation. It was for this that he despised them, so that in his notebook he wrote: 'I see no wit in any of them but Newton. The rest are mere triflers, mere nihilarians' (C 372). It is quite easy to set out the principle of Berkeley's main objection in a form intelligible even to readers who have only the most elementary acquaintance with algebra, and I shall do so by using a simpler example than those Berkeley used and employing a modern notation.

Let us see first how in more recent tradition a simple algebraic differentiation is done from first principles. Let us take the equation

(1) $y = x^2$

which gives y when x is given. Let δx be a small increment to x which gives a small increment δy to y; that is

(2) $y + \delta y = (x + \delta x)^2$.

Then

(3) $y + \delta y = x^2 + 2x\delta x + (\delta x)^2$.

Since $y = x^2$ from (1), this last equation becomes, after subtraction,

(4) $\delta y = 2x\delta x + (\delta x)^2$.

We now divide both sides by δx so that we have

(5) $\dfrac{\delta y}{\delta x} = 2x + \delta x$.

We now say that

(6) the limiting value of $\dfrac{\delta y}{\delta x}$, as δx tends to zero, is $2x$.

What this means is that as the value of δx gets nearer to zero the value of the ratio $\dfrac{\delta y}{\delta x}$ tends to a non-zero limit even though δy and δx both tend to zero. When (6) is true it is customary to write

(7) $\dfrac{dy}{dx} = 2x$.

Here dy and dx are not two mysterious new numbers; (7) is merely the conventional abbreviation of (6). It tells us that if $y = x^2$ then the rate of change of y is twice that of x.

Now if a seventeenth- or early eighteenth-century mathematician were to carry out this differentiation in this notation he would require in the first place that δx should be not merely a small, but an infinitesimally small increment. Berkeley protested that he could not conceive of the infinitesimally small, but that is not now the main point at issue. What is at issue is the move that the old mathematician made after reaching stage (5):

$$(5)\ \frac{\delta y}{\delta x} = 2x + \delta x.$$

He now said that since δx was infinitesimally small it could be neglected, so that we may simple cancel it out to write

$$\star(6)\ \frac{\delta y}{\delta x} = 2x$$

This is the move that aroused Berkeley's derision; if δx could be cancelled it must be a nothing; but to divide δy by nothing or nothing by nothing will never give the result $2x$. The doctrine of the Trinity seemed pellucid to Berkeley by comparison with this piece of argumentation.

It is clear that Berkeley's criticism is irrelevant to more modern presentations and equally clear that it is justified with regard to the type of procedure that we have just considered. There are, indeed, scholarly controversies about whether Newton's later formulations of what we now call the differential calculus are liable to Berkeley's objections; but certainly any formulation which requires us first to posit infinitesimal quantities and then to claim that they can be treated as zero is faulty, and Berkeley was justified in attacking it.

7 Moral and political philosophy

Until very recently, Berkeley's contribution to moral and political philosophy was ignored by, and probably unknown to, all save a few specialists. But, though small in compass, Berkeley's views on these topics are original, clear and concerned with very fundamental issues. As we shall see, one of his achievements was to state with complete clarity a version of utilitarianism which has usually been thought to emerge only gradually in the nineteenth century and to have been stated and distinguished clearly only in the latter part of the twentieth-century.

The only important document we have has the full title: *Passive Obedience or the Christian Doctrine of not Resisting the Supreme Power, Proved and Vindicated upon the Principles of the Law of Nature in a Discourse Delivered at the Chapel of Trinity College, Dublin.* It was published in 1712, between the *Principles* and the *Three Dialogues.* The phrase in the title which runs 'Proved and Vindicated upon the Principles of the Law of Nature' is very important; it indicates that, though the discourse had the form of a sermon on the text 'Whosoever resisteth the Power, resisteth the ordinance of God', the argument is to be based purely on rational, philosophical considerations, with no appeal to authority or revelation. So, at the outset, he says that, in arguing for passive obedience, 'in order to lay the foundation of that duty the deeper, we make some enquiry into the origin, nature and obligation of moral duties in general, and the criterions whereby they are to be known' (O 4).

Every argument must start from premises. Here Berkeley's are first the existence of a good and omnipotent God, which he declares to be evident by the light of nature, and second the principle of self-love. This principle of self-love is the doctrine first stated by the Platonic Socrates and, to the disgust of Bishop Butler, embraced by most subsequent philosophers, that all men always aim at what they take to be most conducive to their happiness. Berkeley, indeed, says that we denominate things good or evil accordingly as they augment or impair our happiness. Since our happiness, our supreme good, must clearly depend on the will of the omnipotent God in the long run, whatever the short-term advantages of disobedience, Berkeley says that 'it plainly follows that a conformity to His will . . . is the sole rule whereby every man who acts up to the principles of reason must govern and square his actions' (O 6).

So the question now is whether, by reason and not by an appeal to revelation, we can know what the will of God is, at least in regard to our actions. Berkeley thinks that we can. Since God is supremely good he will wish the happiness or good of man, and not just of some men but of all men at all times and places. If this is God's will, then we must set ourselves to produce this general good if we are to conform ourselves to the will of God.

The next question, therefore, Berkeley says, is to find how we are to promote this general good that God wills. In order to answer it he starts by making, in paragraph 8, a historically most important distinction between what are now known as act- and rule-utilitarianism, which deserves quotation also for its economical clarity:

The well-being of mankind must necessarily be carried on in one of these two ways:– Either, first, without the injunction of any certain universal rules of morality; only by obliging everyone, upon each particular occasion, to consult the public good, and always to do that which to him shall seem, in the present time and circumstances, most to conduce to it; or, secondly, by enjoining the observation of some determinate, established laws, which if universally practised, have, from the nature of things, an essential fitness to procure the well-being of mankind; though, in their particular application, they are sometimes, through untoward accidents, and the perverse irregularity of human wills, the occasions of great sufferings and misfortunes, it may be, to very many good men.

Berkeley now opts firmly for the second method, which we now call rule-utilitarianism. Act-utilitarians protest that, if one is sure that violation of some traditional rule of morality will have the best results, then it is mere conditioned rule-worship

to obey the rule; in cases of uncertainty, they will often concede, it is best to act in the way which in most similar circumstances has usually turned out to be for the best, but this is to
treat the traditional rules as rules of thumb, prudential maxims,
and not to allow them authority, as does the rule-utilitarian.

But Berkeley argues that, first, we have neither the knowledge
nor the time to judge of the basic merits of an action, whereas it
is easy to determine that it is a case of lying or theft, and,
secondly, we need public standards of behaviour to give certainty to our judgements about what is permissible and what requires prohibition. Without general rules of conduct of manage-
able complexity 'there ensues the most horrible confusion of
vice and virtue, sin and duty that can possibly be imagined' (O
10).

So we must, thinks Berkeley, conclude that the general welfare, which is willed by God, can best be achieved by recognition of determinate rules; 'whatever practical proposition doth
to right reason evidently appear to have a necessary connexion
with the Universal well-being included in it, is to be looked
upon as enjoined by the will of God' (O 11). In general, he
holds, these principles are evident to all men; they are eternal
rules of reason and should be adhered to even when such desirable human feelings as tenderness and benevolence speak
against so doing. To use an illustration drawn from Hume,
though we all dislike the thought of a deserving poor man
paying a debt to a rich miser, none the less, the principle of
justice must prevail.

We have reached the conclusion that 'the Law of Nature is a
system of such rules or precepts as that, if they be all of them,
at all times, in all places, and by all men observed, they will
necessarily promote the well-being of mankind, so far as it is
attainable by human actions' (O 11). There are 'unalterable
moral rules, which to violate to the least degree is vice or sin'
(O 15). We all know what these rules are; Berkeley gives as
examples 'Thou shalt not forswear thyself' and 'Thou shalt not
steal', among others.

That is the moral theory put forward by Berkeley. It is on
this basis that he has to defend and explain the principle of
passive obedience. In modern times, when the question of the

limits of civil obedience is often discussed, it is of interest to see how Berkeley attempted to defend this extreme position by rational argument and without appeal to such extravagant notions as the divine right of kings, which has been employed by his Jacobite predecessors.

Berkeley starts by stressing the miseries of anarchy. Hobbes had said that in a state of nature, which is a state of anarchy, we find 'no arts, no letters, no society, and, which is worst of all, continual fear and danger of sudden death, and the life of man solitary, poor, nasty, brutish, and short'. Berkeley echoes this; without the law of society 'there is no politeness, no order, no peace, among men, but the world is one great heap of misery and confusion' (O 15). So obedience to the law of society, and thus to those who make and enforce the law, is of the highest importance and cannot be left to individual discretion. Obedience is 'a rule of law of nature, the least breach whereof hath the inherent stain of moral turpitude'. Breaches of obedience lead to the dissolution of society with all its attendant evils.

The remainder of the discourse is devoted to defending this doctrine and explaining it. We shall consider only two points. First, Berkeley acknowledges that lawful authority may order one to act in a way that transgresses moral law; in such a case the principle of non-resistance does not require us so to act; but it does require us not to resist any penalty that the authority may impose on us if we do in these circumstances fail to comply. Berkeley bases this claim on a distinction that he makes between positive and negative precepts, only the latter of which have totally binding force. This is not an easy distinction to understand. If we take 'negative' and 'positive' to refer to mere grammatical form the distinction is untenable, since the positive 'Always tell the truth' has the same effect as 'Never lie.' On the other hand it does seem intuitively that there is a distinction between abstaining from thwarting the will and needs of others and actively co-operating with them. There is room for debate.

The second point to notice is that Berkeley agrees that 'by virtue of the duty of non-resistance we are not obliged to submit the disposal of our lives and fortunes to the discretion either of madmen, or of all those who by craft or violence invade the supreme power' (O 52). This is surely dangerous, and would not have been tolerated by Hobbes. Berkeley was loyal to the newly reigning house of Hanover: but might not a Jacobite have claimed that Berkeley's caveat justified him in rebellion? It is very hard for those who claim that there are principles which should absolutely never be transgressed to avoid both the Scylla of carrying it to absurdity (such as obeying a madman) and the Charybdis of inserting qualifying clauses that rob it of certainty of interpretation.

Finally, Berkeley was a sincerely religious man. He wished to propagate the Christian religion both because he thought it true and from a religious concern for the souls of men. But he also, as we have seen, makes it the basis of morality. We, who aim at our own happiness, are to aim at the general happiness that is willed by God because it is only by obeying the will of God that we can achieve our own happiness. So Berkeley thinks that without religion men have no rational motive to be moral; and since political obedience has a moral justification, the atheist will also have no inner drive to obedience but only at most fear of retribution from the civil power. So for Berkeley our temporal as well as our spiritual well-being is based only in religion. We find in Berkeley's apologetic writings, such as *Alciphron*, a continual awareness of and stress on the practical importance of combating atheism. Within limits Berkeley was an advocate of religious toleration; there exists an episcopal charge to the clergy of the diocese of Cloyne, which he delivered as Bishop, in which he exhorts them to friendship with and understanding of the many Catholics who surrounded them. But there could be no toleration for atheists, since they had no rational motive for the preservation of moral society, as did all theists, however misguided in their theological views. So, in his *Discourse Addressed to Magistrates and Men in Authority*, Berkeley warns them that 'obedience to all civil power is rooted in the religious fear of God'; so they should be aware that 'those pretended advocates for private light and free thought are in reality seditious men, who set up themselves against national laws and constitutions' (L vi 208). Magistrates, he concludes, should enforce the law against them.

The most important of Berkeley's views were formed, and the most important and enduring of his works were written, while he was a young Fellow of Trinity College, Dublin. *An Essay Towards a New Theory of Vision* had appeared in 1709, the *Principles* in 1710, *Passive Obedience* in 1712 and the *Three Dialogues* in 1713. Berkeley, as we shall see, published many further works in later life, some of which then made more stir by far than those we have mentioned. But today it is only the *De motu* of 1721 which is regarded as adding significantly to the previously mentioned publications.

The remainder of Berkeley's works were written against a background of more practical interests and were often directed more to religious and social than to philosophical ends. After writing the *Three Dialogues* Berkeley left Dublin for London in 1713 on leave, and though he was to remain a Fellow for some years he never resumed active work at Trinity College.

In London Berkeley met some of the foremost literary figures of the day. These included Steele, to whose *Guardian* Berkeley contributed a few articles, Pope, who presented Berkeley with a copy of his poem 'Windsor Forest', and Addison. He became closely associated with his fellow-Irishman Swift, and through him with Mrs Vanhomrigh, the mother of Swift's Vanessa. There was to be a curious sequel to this: Vanessa had intended to make Swift her heir, but, angered by his marriage to Stella, she changed her will and left a large legacy to Berkeley instead, though she had never met him, a legacy which Berkeley received in 1723 when Vanessa died.

But Berkeley was not satisfied by his reception in London, for it was not literary friendships but recognition of his philosophy that he was seeking, and this eluded him. Already, before his arrival in London, his influential friend Sir John Percival had warned him in a letter of what was to come: 'I did but name the subject-matter of your *Principles* to some ingenuous friends of mine, and they immediately treated it with ridicule, at the same time refusing to read it; which I have not yet got one to do.' On arrival Berkeley was faced with the same difficulty; the London intelligentsia to whom he had looked for comment and reasoned argument welcomed the man but refused even to discuss his views with him.

So Berkeley was not happy in London. In 1713 he took the opportunity to become chaplain to Lord Peterborough and toured France and Italy with him in that year and in 1714, and after another two years in London returned to Italy in 1716 for an extended tour which lasted until 1720. Berkeley wrote a journal on this tour, of which a portion dealing with the year 1717 survives. It was towards the end of this tour that he wrote his Latin treatise on mechanics, *De motu*, which he published on his return to England.

Berkeley returned to Dublin in 1721 and received the degree of Doctor of Divinity. But he was no longer happy in either Ireland or England, both of which he found decadent and corrupt, as such of his writings as *An Essay towards Preventing the Ruin of Great Britain* (1721) abundantly show. In 1723 he wrote to Lord Percival: 'It is now about ten months since I have determined to spend the residue of my days in Bermuda, where I trust in Providence I may be the mean instument of doing good to mankind'; he added that a number of his friends were determined to go with him. The good that he proposed to do to mankind is made clear by the full title of a publication of 1725: *A proposal for the better supplying of Churches in our Foreign Plantations, and for converting the savage Americans to Christianity, by a College to be erected in the Summer Islands, otherwise called the Isles of Bermuda.*

In 1724 Berkeley was made Dean of Derry, but this seems to have had no effect on his plans, for he never took up residence in Derry, though nominally Dean until 1734. In 1724 he went to London to whip up support for the Bermuda project and, so far as words went, received strong backing for his impractical and unresearched project. Many private persons promised donations, the House of Commons voted a grant of twenty thousand pounds, George I gave Berkeley a charter for the college, and Walpole himself promised support. But little came of this promised aid; the parliamentary grant was delayed and Walpole temporised.

So Berkeley lost patience and in 1728, having married, he took ship for America. 'Westward the course of empire takes its way', he wrote in his only known poem, and Berkeley accompanied it. He landed at Newport in Rhode Island and, after a short stay there, bought a farm outside Newport and built a house which he called Whitehall. The house still stands and, after a period of neglect, was renovated and reopened to the public in 1980. Berkeley appears to have been happy and well liked in Rhode Island. He made contact with Yale College in New Haven and had close contacts with Samuel Johnson, a missionary living in Stratford, who, with Jonathan Edwards, became one of the first two American philosophers of note. Some of Berkeley's correspondence with Johnson survives, and that part in which he explains problems about the *Principles* to Johnson is useful reading. In Rhode Island Berkeley also wrote *Alciphron*, a philosophical defence of Christianity against freethinkers. There is little in this work which still has philosophical or religious importance, though there are occasional passages, such as that in which Berkeley discusses how an empiricist can claim to know what he means by grace, which the specialist must read.

But Berkeley was living in virtual retirement, not carrying out his philanthropic projects. By 1731 Walpole had made it clear that the government support which Berkeley needed would not be forthcoming. So in 1732 Berkeley gave the many books he had taken out with him for his new college to Yale College instead and returned to England, defeated. He never set foot on Bermuda.

In 1734 Berkeley was appointed Bishop of Cloyne in the south of Ireland. Unlike the Deanery of Derry, Berkeley did not regard the bishopric as a sinecure. He went straight to live in his diocese and remained there continuously until just before his death. He appears to have been a dutiful diocesan bishop with a particular interest in trying to promote harmony between the established Church of Ireland, to which he belonged, and the more numerous Catholics of that part of Ireland. One of his writings of the period is addressed to the Catholic clergy in most conciliatory terms asking for their support in improving the economic welfare of Ireland.

Berkeley was much exercised by the very poor economic state of Ireland compared with most continental countries and with England. This backwardness he attributed partly to the laziness and ignorance of the peasant population, partly to the excessive number of absentee landlords who drained the country of its wealth while contributing nothing, and partly to an unnecessary excess of imports over exports. Berkeley exposed the facts and proposed some remedies in a work called the *Querist* which was published in three parts in 1735, 1736 and 1737. Unlike most of his writings the *Querist* makes laborious reading, especially since it takes the form of some six hundred separate numbered queries. Its intention was practical, but certain theoretical economic positions are implicit in Berkeley's criticisms and proposals, and it is thus his main contribution to economics.

The importance of work for wealth is one of Berkeley's main themes. It is to be found in the first query: 'Whether there ever was, is, or will be, an industrious nation poor or an idle rich?', and it recurs over and over again. Another main theme is that money is important only as an instrument of exchange and that gold and silver are of little value. 'Whether there be any virtue in gold or silver, other than as they set people at work, or create industry?', Berkeley asks, and 'Whether the denominations being retained, although the bullion were gone, things might not nevertheless be rated, bought and sold, industry promoted, and a circulation of commerce maintained?' (Queries 30, 26). But though he stressed the connection between labour and wealth, Berkeley was well aware of the importance of the market place for determining value. Query 24 runs: 'Whether the value or price of things be not a compounded proportion, directly as the demand, and reciprocally as the plenty?'

Berkeley was on the whole in favour of restricting foreign trade, largely because he thought it criminal to send abroad Irish food to import such things as French brandy when the peasants were starving. So he asks 'whether trade be not then on a right foot, when foreign commodities are imported in exchange only for domestic superfluities?' (Query 172). He goes on to ask 'whether there should not be published yearly schedules of our trade, containing an account of the imports and exports of the foregoing year?' (Query 179).

Berkeley was also much impressed with the importance of banks, thinking it 'the greatest help and spur to commerce that property can be so readily conveyed and so well secured by a *compte en banc*, that is, by only writing one man's name for another's in the bank-book' (Query 296). Banks promoted trade and he·was convinced that it was necessary to establish a bank of Ireland, a national bank on the model of those in Venice, Hamburg and Amsterdam, cities whose wealth Berkeley attributed largely to their public banks. While it is hard to claim that Berkeley ranks with Hume and Adam Smith in importance as a philosophical economist, historians of that science regard him as a significant figure.

The two works for which Berkeley was best known in his own day were published while he was Bishop of Cloyne. We have considered *The Analyst* (1734) in the chapter on Berkeley's views on mathematics. In the following year he published replies to attacks on *The Analyst*, including the amusingly titled *Reasons for not Replying to Mr Walton's Full Answer*.

But something more must be said of *Siris: A Chain of Philosophical Reflexions and Inquiries concerning the Virtues of Tarwater, and divers other subjects connected together and arising one from another*, published in 1744. This was Berkeley's last published work apart from some letters about the virtues of tarwater and *Farther Thoughts on Tar-water*, published in 1752: the word *Siris*, derived from a Greek word meaning 'chain', is explained by the rest of the title. Starting from a consideration of the virtues of tar-water as a medicine and questions about its best method of manufacture, Berkeley goes on to consider more generally the nature of the physical universe, of the spiritual universe and, finally, of God. In the course of the discussions much curious learning is exhibited concerning Pythagoras, Plato, Aristotle, Theophrastus, Plotinus, Iamblichus and other ancient thinkers.

Berkeley believed that tar-water was a panacea. He had first come across it when in America, particularly as a remedy for smallpox. It was a concoction formed by boiling up in water the tar exuded from the incised bark of pine or fir trees; Berkeley directs that it should be drunk by the glassful. He tried the remedy on his local Irish population for smallpox, ulcers, consumptive cough, erysipelas, indigestion and asthma with uniformly beneficial results. The nerves constitute the inner garment of the soul, and thus the oil in tar-water can act beneficially on the mind also.

It was as providing a medical panacea that Berkeley's *Siris* attracted so much attention, though the medical fraternity appears not to have been unduly impressed. It is doubtful if much more of the work was read then, and few read any of it now; yet its editor A. C. Fraser calls it 'the consummation, on the basis of ancient philosophy, of Berkeley's conception of the concrete universe, past present and future, as in necessary dependence upon all-constitutive Intelligence'. Certainly there are passages, one or two of which have been quoted in earlier chapters, which do help to explain and enlarge Berkeley's analytic and metaphysical views of science. But though Berkeley certainly maintains the immaterialism of his earlier philosophy there is now a strain of speculative metaphysics which seems quite alien to the earlier Berkeley. Here is a specimen (S 171): 'The tunicle of the soul, whether it be called pure aether, or luciform vehicle, or animal spirit, seemeth to be that which acts upon the gross organs, as it is determined by the soul from which it immediately receives impression.' He goes on to say that 'some moderns have thought fit to deride all that is said of aetherial vehicles, as mere jargon or words without a meaning'. The early Berkeley who wrote: 'Mem. To be eternally banishing metaphysics, &c., and recalling men to Common Sense' (C 751) might have thought aetherial vehicles in no better condition than matter.

Berkeley continued to live in his diocese until 1752, when he retired to Oxford, where he had a son at Christ Church. He took a house in Holywell Street. On the evening of Sunday 14 January 1753, while listening to his wife reading from the Bible, he died suddenly. Perhaps he had a fear of being buried alive; he certainly expressed a wish in his will that he should not be buried until there were signs of bodily corruption. He was accordingly buried on the following Saturday. His grave can still be seen in the floor of the nave of Christ Church cathedral. There is a memorial tablet on a pillar close by; its eulogy of Berkeley's character and intellectual gifts is accurate; its dating of his birth is not.

9 Critical retrospect

The aim of this book has been to describe the life and works of Berkeley, not to defend them or adversely criticise them, though there has been no rigorous avoidance of expressions of praise and agreement or of condemnation and disagreement. But since it has so often been said that Berkeley's views are impossible to accept and impossible to refute, the reader might welcome a final critical evaluation of his main position.

There are two main premises of Berkeley's philosophy. One of them is that all that is ever before the mind is ideas, ideas being taken to cover both perception and thought and to be mental images. The second is one of the many theses which have been called the principle of empiricism. Berkeley stated it at least twice in his notebooks; he said: 'Foolish in men to despise the senses. If it were not for them the mind could have no knowledge, no thought at all'; and again: 'I approve of this axiom of the Schoolmen, "Nihil est in intellectu quod non prius fuit in sensu" [Nothing is in the intellect which was not previously in sensation]' (C 539, 779).

It is surely clear that if both these premises of Berkeley are correct then his main contention that matter is unthinkable must also be correct. For the relevant concept of matter is of something that is never an object of the senses and so never in the intellect. If empiricism as Berkeley states it is correct then we can think only of the ideas that are the sole objects of the mind. So it does not matter much what we think of the detail of some of his argument, which varies in quality; we must either deny one or both of these premises or accept the conclusion.

It is far from clear that either of these premises is correct. Let us first consider briefly the premise that all objects of perception are ideas, thought of as mental images, caused by matter, according to Locke, or by God directly, according to Berkeley. Berkeley had claimed that Locke's ontology was inflated, and that this unintelligible matter was unnecessary; why should God use matter or any other instrument in his government of the world? So Locke requires God to create and control matter, matter to cause ideas, ideas to be the content of minds, and minds to receive them. Berkeley cuts out matter from the chain. Both are equally in disagreement with pre-philosophical common belief; for in most people's thought there is, maybe, God to create and sustain, there are physical bodies, and there are minds which observe the bodies. There is neither the matter which Berkeley rejected, nor the ideas of sense which he accepted. Certainly Berkeley does not deny that there are in some sense physical bodies, but they are hypothetical constructs and not the direct objects of perception.

It is by no means clear that the arguments against the common pre-philosophical beliefs are good ones. Berkeley relies principally on the so-called argument from illusion, on such facts as that water can feel hot to one hand and cold to another and that a penny will look a different shape from different angles. But it is not clear that these are good reasons for claiming that bodies are not directly perceived. It might be instructive for the reader to consider, if the facts of perspective tell against direct perception of objects, how a penny would have to look if it were directly perceived. Would it always look round, and, if so, how could he distinguish it visually from a sphere?

It is also not clear why, if we believe that we perceive physical bodies, we should think of matter as something distinct from them and lurking behind them. It might be thought that the scientific description of the world is an alternative description of the world we perceive rather than a description of another world. If it is an alternative description of the world we perceive it is not clear why we should think of ourselves as being obliged to ask whether the everyday description of the world or the scientific description is *the* correct one. There are many alternative and equally correct descriptions of each of us, for example, which vary only in their utility in various contexts. It is far from clear that when one says that a tomato is red one is saying anything which is in intention or in fact incompatible with scientific theories about matter, colour or anything else, so why need we choose one or the other?

So, while these few comments have obviously not refuted

Berkeley's view that the sole objects of perception are ideas, we should at least not accept it without discussion or agree with him that, as he claims in the very first line of the *Principles*, it is evident that ideas are the sole objects of human knowledge.

It is also far from clear that the empiricist thesis as formulated by Berkeley is acceptable. It is not merely that there are some concepts, of traditional concern to philosophers, such as those of necessity, of matter, of God, of force or of goodness, which have often been regarded as examples of what must be treated as innate ideas or a priori concepts. This extreme empiricist doctrine seems to be unable to account for various plebeian concepts which it would be absurd to regard as a priori. Thus we might consider the concept of a trump, as it occurs in bridge. It seems clear that there is no sensible mark of being a trump which distinguishes it from other cards as there is a conspicuous mark of a spade which distinguishes it from other cards; so the concept of a trump cannot reach us from our senses as Berkeley claims is the case with all concepts. It is also very difficult to see how we could think about trumps in non-verbal ideas; we cannot concentrate our attention on any sensible feature in order to do so, for being a trump involves no distinctive sensible feature. It is easy to see that the same considerations apply to the concepts of an uncle, a felony, or of limited liability; with a little deeper thought it can be seen that the same applies to nearly all concepts.

So Berkeley has surely relied on a defective concept of empiricism in order to justify his claim that the concept of matter is unintelligible. It may well be that there is some other principle of empiricism which Berkeley could invoke to yield him the desired conclusion, but we cannot agree that Berkeley has clearly proved his contention.

But if Berkeley's arguments are not conclusive, they are by no means without value. Locke's views are very attractive to educated people with some knowledge of science; they swept Europe in the eighteenth century and they are probably held in some nebulous form by many people in the twentieth century. Locke was a less extreme empiricist than Berkeley, but possibly at the expense of some inconsistency, for at times he certainly seems to accept those empiricist premises that Berkeley accepted and whose self-evidence we have just called into question. It is a genuine question whether views like those of Locke are safe from the type of criticism that Berkeley had to offer.

But Berkeley was not merely destructive. In his own time, to Berkeley's intense indignation, his denial of matter was treated by most as a form of that scepticism which he claimed to demolish. There were indeed few in the eighteenth century who made any serious attempt to understand him. Hume (of whose work Berkeley appears to have been entirely ignorant) appreciated and understood him, but this is true of few others. Kant, without reading him, claimed to refute him in a 'Refutation of Idealism' which is a model of impenetrable obscurity, and it is typical of the attitude of the nineteenth century that in Ueberweg's monumental *History of Philosophy*, published at the end of the century, Berkeley is granted only a few words in the course of a chapter largely devoted to Locke.

But this view of Berkeley, based largely on ignorance, is quite wrong. His editor, A. C. Fraser, one of the first to appreciate his true worth, was surely right to place him with Hume and Kant as one of the three great philosophers of the eighteenth century. Unfortunately the view of Berkeley as merely a propounder of a paradoxical theory of perception has lingered on in the twentieth century. But his worth has been recognised more and more, and few who have read him with care would deny his importance in the philosophy of science or the brilliance of his many insights in other areas of philosophy. His position as one of the most gifted and most readable of philosophers is now secure.

Further reading

The Works of George Berkeley, Bishop of Cloyne, edited by A. A. Luce and T. E. Jessop, 9 vols. Nelson and Sons, Edinburgh, 1948–57, is the most complete and accurate presentation of all Berkeley's writings.

Berkeley's Complete Works, edited by A. C. Fraser, 4 vols, Oxford at the Clarendon Press, 1901, is not so complete but contains all the major works.

There are paperback editions of the *New Theory of Vision*, the *Principles* and the *Three Dialogues between Hylas and Philonous*, singly or in various combinations, in abundance.

Berkeley by George Pitcher, Routledge & Kegan Paul, London, 1977, is the best large-scale study of Berkeley available.

Berkeley by G. J. Warnock, Pelican, Harmondsworth, 1953, is a good shorter treatment concentrating on the main themes of the *Principles*.

Locke and Berkeley: A Collection of Critical Essays, edited by C. B. Martin and D. M. Armstrong, Macmillan, London, n.d., is a very useful collection which reprints some of the most important modern articles on Berkeley.

Index